DONE HUNTING

a memoir

MARTIN HUNTER

ECW PRESS

Published by ECW Press
665 Gerrard Street East
Toronto, Ontario, Canada, M4M 1Y2
416-694-3348 / info@ecwpress.com

To the best of his abilities, the author has related experiences, places, people, and organizations from his memories of them.

The publication of *Done Hunting* has been generously supported by the Government of Canada through the Canada Book Fund. *Ce livre est financé en partie par le gouvernement du Canada.*

Canada

LIBRARY AND ARCHIVES CANADA
CATALOGUING IN PUBLICATION

Hunter, Martin, 1933-, author
Done hunting : a memoir / Martin Hunter.

Issued in print and electronic formats.
ISBN 978-1-77041-329-0 (paperback)
ALSO ISSUED AS: 978-1-77090-936-6 (PDF)
978-1-77090-935-9 (EPUB)

1. Hunter, Martin, 1933–. 2. Dramatists, Canadian (English)—20th century—Biography. 3. Toronto (Ont.)—Biography.

I. Title.

PS8565.U58Z46 2016 C812'.54 C2016-902334-6
C2016-902335-4

Editor for the press: Michael Holmes
Text design: Stan Bevington
Cover image: Richard Williams

PRINTING: COACH HOUSE PRINTING 5 4 3 2 1
PRINTED AND BOUND IN CANADA

CONTENTS

LOLLING IN LOTUS LAND 1

JOHNNY BANANAS 19

MOVIE MADNESS 28

SCHOOL FOR GOSSIPS 36

NASTY SURPRISE 45

SERENDIPITY IN SWEDEN 58

RADIO DAYS 74

DOWN MEXICO WAY 91

UP AND DOWN IN LONDON, PARIS, AND TORONTO 99

THE STRATFORD EXPERIENCE 108

ESCAPADE 118

GOD SAVE THE FOUNDATION 129

LOVERS AND MADMEN 139

NO FOOL LIKE AN OLD FOOL 149

THE TENNESSEE WALTZ 157

COASTING 168

What is love, 'tis not hereafter;
Present mirth hath present laughter;
What's to come is still unsure . . . .

William Shakespeare, *Twelfth Night*

This book is dedicated to my brother Bill,
who appears rarely in these pages,
in gratitude for his continuing encouragement
and support.

Cover drawing by my long-time friend
Richard Williams.

LOLLING IN LOTUS LAND

Flying across the Rockies as the setting sun gilded their snow-capped peaks and landing at the Vancouver airport just as the lights began to come on all across the city, I felt the promise of new beginnings, new adventures. I took a taxi to the house that Laurier LaPierre was renting with some friends in English Bay and was welcomed with a shot of whisky and a quizzical grin.

"'Ow nice to see you, mon cher. You look sexier than evair." He introduced his housemates: my friend Bill Glassco's cousin Chris Price, and a pretty young boy of twenty-two named Kevin who was trying to recover from a recent breakup with his boyfriend. We tucked into some smoked salmon and then sat down to a splendid meal: lamb ragout and braised parsnips, followed by crème brûlée. I had forgotten what an accomplished cook Laurier was.

I had returned to Toronto after a round-the-world tour hoping to find work as a theatre director; it was what I had done for the previous ten years. But I found that working as a freelancer was not easy. Unless you were a promising kid with a pretty face, you were expected to have a theatre of your own so you could reciprocate by offering theatre directors a show in your space. Besides, after ten years at the university I was labelled an "academic" director, whatever that was supposed to mean.

Then I learned that Ryerson Community College, as it was then known, was looking for a new head of their theatre department. I was summoned to meet a panel, one of whose members was a former student with whom I had always gotten along well. He was very encouraging, and I thought the interview had gone well. A few weeks later I received a letter informing me that although they thought I was qualified, they had interviewed another applicant who had an Oxford degree, so of course I would understand that they considered him preferable.

I learned that Christopher Newton was leaving the Vancouver Playhouse to become the leader of the Shaw Festival, and the Playhouse was looking for a new artistic director. I sent in an application and received an enthusiastic reply explaining that the board would be very interested in meeting me. I decided to fly to Vancouver at my own expense to show my enthusiasm. Did I want to move to Vancouver? I had only the briefest acquaintance with the city, gained during a weekend on leave when I was a naval cadet back in the 1950s, but I had heard good things about the coastal city and had several friends and acquaintances there. It would be a chance to remake myself in a new environment and I was determined to grasp the opportunity.

The interview with the board members was courteous. The chairman was an Englishman with a neatly trimmed moustache, who peered at me over his half-glasses. There were two or three men in business suits and half a dozen women, all smartly dressed.

"Tell us a little bit about yourself," said the chairman.

I explained that I had been a child actor, had played leading roles at university, and studied briefly at the LAMDA in London.

"Why did you come to Canada?" asked one of the women. She was a big woman, big hair, big lips, big breasts, and no doubt a big bum.

"I was born here."

"So you're a Canadian. How amusing." A slight titter went around the table.

"From your résumé, you seem to have mainly directed classical texts. Shakespeare, Molière, the Greeks."

"I've done a number of Canadian plays by James Reaney, Robertson Davies, Angus Braid . . ."

"Braid? Should we know him?"

"A very talented young writer. One of my former students."

"Ah, a student." Her breasts heaved as she turned to signal the chairman her dismissal of this minor accomplishment.

"Do you have any experience with musicals?"

"I turned a number of classical texts into musicals. Works by Brecht, Aristophanes, Wedekind . . ."

"Pardon my ignorance. Who is Wedekind?"

"An Austrian writer of the early twentieth century. He wrote the Lulu plays that formed the basis of the opera by Alban Berg."

"Your interests seem rather esoteric, if you don't mind me saying so," volunteered a rather acid-faced woman in a pinstriped pantsuit. "What about comedy? Do you have any experience directing comedy? Audiences like to be amused."

"I've directed comedies by Shakespeare, Garrick, Alexander Pope, Edward Albee."

"What about Neil Simon?"

"Well, no . . ."

"Your experience strikes me as rather academic," said one of the businessmen.

"I was working for a university."

"Of course."

I realized I was losing their interest. The interview went on for perhaps another ten minutes before the chairman thanked me and said they would be in touch. Then he shot his final salvo: "What a pity you're not English." I was not surprised that I didn't get the job.

The next day I visited my friend Tony Bourne, who lived in a neat little apartment in English Bay. He had been in my year in Trinity and after failing first year three times had been told that he was not suited to academic study. He took a job in advertising in Montreal for a while and then drifted west where he settled with his mother, who lived in an apartment on the floor above him. Another friend described her as "a sweet English rose who had been insufficiently watered." Mother and son dined together most evenings, though they no longer dressed for dinner as they had done when Tony's father, who had been a colonel of the Shanghai police before the war, was still alive.

After dinner Tony sometimes went out on the town visiting gay bars, where he had an extensive acquaintance. He was not a serious drinker, but even so I could not understand where he got the money to do this. He did work several afternoons a week for an antique dealer, but I think his mother must have given him an allowance. As the widow of a British officer she would have had a meagre pension, but perhaps she had inherited some family money. After a typically English meal of overdone beef, boiled potatoes, and Brussels sprouts, Tony turned to me, "Carpe diem, carpe balls. Let's head to the Castle."

In the bar at the Castle Hotel, a long-time gay hangout, we encountered Tony's friend Arthur, an enormous and genial Native Canadian. Tony confided later that Arthur was an aristocrat in whatever tribe he belonged to, where he had a rank roughly equivalent to the Duke of Edinburgh.

Arthur was a well-known figure in the Vancouver gay community. Two years earlier he had been crowned Empress of the Pacific Northwest at the annual drag ball. Tony, Arthur, and I were to spend several evenings together.

Arthur was quick-witted but not malicious, and he pointed out a number of prominent Vancouver gays, commenting on their entertainment value and sexual endowment and proficiency. He suggested we round off the evening with a visit to the baths but we declined.

The next evening Chris Price and Laurier took me to hear their friend June Katz, a jazz singer at a local bistro. June was a New Yorker and a divorcee, a handsome woman with a smoky voice and a style reminiscent of Billie Holiday. She sang several standards; I particularly remember her rendition of "Don't Smoke in Bed." In between sets she came to our table, and we immediately clicked. We made a date to have lunch the next day in her house at Point Grey.

June's other luncheon guest was her friend Emmanuelle Gattuso, an equally lively woman, who drove up in a rickety old Mercedes. We all drank martinis and ate lobster sandwiches. Emmanuelle reported that she had started dating a very rich man but wasn't sure whether it was leading anywhere. June encouraged her to keep on; her own boyfriend was far from perfect, but she couldn't imagine not having a man in her life. She was still on very good terms with her ex-husband. "He's a sweetheart. I wish I was still in love with him, but what can you do? I just knew it was time to move on."

After lunch, they suggested we go to Wreck Beach. We drove in the Mercedes to the UBC campus, parked, and went down a steep wooden stairway to the beach below. It turned out to be a nude beach, populated by people of all ages walking around in the buff. There were some very attractive young people but also people in their forties, fifties, and even sixties. We all shed our clothes and set out on a walk to admire the eye candy.

I found myself being ogled by a rather fleshy young woman in her twenties. I encouraged June and Emmanuelle to go off on a stroll on their own and the young woman came over and introduced herself as Melissa. She told me she was a student of anthropology and asked me if I had seen the museum of native artifacts on the university campus. When I replied in the negative, she offered to give me a tour the next afternoon. I was to meet her at the entrance at one o'clock. She gave me an appraising look and took off when she saw June and Emmanuelle coming back. "Good for you. You scored!" crowed June, with a knowing grimace.

The next afternoon I waited for Melissa. Outside the museum were tall totems, carved by the various tribes of the West Coast. I had seen totem poles at the museum in Toronto but they were encased in stairwells. Here they stood in the open air, majestic against a background of distant mountains and forests. I had a sense of the mystery of an ancient culture.

Melissa was a bit late, but when she showed up she took me inside the museum, which displayed the fantastic brightly painted masks the native people had carved to be used in their rituals. Melissa explained that they danced in these masks, which represented the spirit of the animals associated with the various tribes. Each tribe had a winter potlatch, a feast at which they gave each other gifts. The grander the gift, the greater the status of the giver. Unfortunately, this tradition led to the destruction of native society. With the coming of the white man, the chiefs aspired to give even more magnificent gifts: top hats, bathtubs, copper spittoons.

In order to afford these luxuries, they sent their women into the cities of Vancouver and Victoria to work as prostitutes. Many of them contracted diseases, which they brought home, which rapidly decimated the native population. The native societies, which had survived more or less intact until nearly the end of the nineteenth century, collapsed. Early in the twentieth century, the Canadian government banned the potlatches and confiscated many of the masks and other regalia associated with the ceremonies. They took them to Ottawa and sold many of them, reportedly for a few thousand dollars, to the Museum of Natural History in New York, where they can still be seen gathering dust in the basement, although the Canadian government kept some of the best items, which are now proudly displayed at the Canadian Museum of History in Gatineau.

I was fascinated by these expressive masks and painted boxes. I had always been interested in Aboriginal culture, beginning with the displays in the basement of the Royal Ontario Museum where, in glass cases, models of native communities were set up with mannequins clothed in fringed and beaded buckskin, squatting around fires or sewing leather leggings and moccasins. But this was another world altogether, a world that took shape in dense forests by the Pacific shore. These native people went to sea in huge war canoes and the museum actually had some early bits of film showing these activities.

As we lay together in her bed in her room in a campus residence, I asked Melissa if I could visit some of the native communities. She told me they still performed some of the ceremonies but because they had been banned it was hard for white men to gain access to them. However, she had been asked to accompany a small ship on an expedition up the channel between the mainland and Vancouver Island and possibly up to Haida country in the Queen Charlotte Islands. She and one of her fellow graduate students were to be the resident experts on the voyage. She would see if there was any chance that I could be included as a passenger.

A few days later, I took Tony and his mother to lunch at a restaurant at the Sylvia Hotel. This slightly faded establishment on the edge of Stanley Park was the choice of Mrs. Bourne, who recalled having tea there when she first came to Canada and was entertained by some other Englishwomen just before the outbreak of war in 1939. "Of course I had no idea what lay ahead, but I think my husband knew. He had arranged to ship some of our furniture out here because he thought we might be staying a bit longer than expected. I had wanted to bring Tony's *ayah* with us, because of course he had spent more time with her than with me. I'm afraid we Englishwomen were rather frivolous. We played bridge three afternoons a week and dined out almost every night."

"Mother was known as the Rose of Shanghai. And she actually met Mrs. Simpson."

"Don't be silly, Tony. She merely happened to be at the same hotel one night on the Bund. They had the best jazz band in the city. All Chinese. Your father and I loved to dance. And she was there with a couple of rather loud American men. Tycoons, I should imagine. We would certainly not have agreed to be introduced to her, even though it was before she got her hooks into that poor, deluded young man, the Prince of Wales. He broke his mother's heart."

"Wasn't his mother the one who forced him to abdicate?"

"I really wouldn't know, dear. We were off in the Pacific and terribly out of touch. My husband thought he should have been horse-whipped. If the old King was still alive, he would have been. But then the war came along, and thank God for George VI. Fortunately, we had taken long leave before the Japanese invaded China. Once war broke out, my husband went to Washington to work for the Embassy as a military attaché and I put you boys in school. You were very young, barely eight, but you would have been sent home to England in a year or so anyway. Probably to Marlborough. That was your father's school. And I felt Robin would look out for you at Ridley."

Robin was Tony's brother, and Tony had lived much of his childhood in

Robin's shadow. Robin had excelled in games but although Tony made his mark as a gymnast and played the female lead in the school play, he did not become a prefect. Robin went on to the Royal Military College in Kingston, married the Commandant's daughter, and eventually became a colonel. "His father was really quite proud of him, although of course he never let on," Mrs. Bourne recalled. "I'm sure he would have done very well in England."

The Bournes felt they were carrying on the best of English tradition in darkest Canada. Tony tried to emulate English social manners of the early twentieth century, where his relatives rode to hounds and danced the night away at debutante balls, although he had only once been to England, for two weeks.

"Dear Tony would have had compatible contemporaries in London who would have introduced him to the right sort of young people. Still, I'm so glad he has you as a friend. I understand you are staying with a television producer, Mr. LaPierre? Tony said he has seen him on the telly. I watch one soap opera every afternoon. Occasionally Tony and I watch it together, don't we, my darling?"

"When I'm not working, Mummy."

"He explains what's happening to me. I get rather muddled, you know. Tony does try to keep his end up, but it's difficult for him. Fortunately, he has an eye for what's really good. Not that most of the things in his shop are first rate. I don't suppose there's any chance that you could introduce him to your television friend? I've always thought Tony might do rather well in that field."

I promised Mrs. Bourne I would see what I could do and she set off back to their apartment building a few blocks away.

Tony and I went for a walk along the seawall around Stanley Park. The great conifers towered above and the waves washed in just below the path. The air was heavy with the smell of the giant evergreens and the salty tang of the ocean. We paused at Second Beach. "If you follow that trail you'll run into quite a few men cruising for sex, some of them quite young and handsome," Tony said. "I'd go in with you, but you'd probably do better on your own."

"Thanks for the tip, but I think I'll pass."

"Let's go on then. There's a little place where we could have tea."

When I spoke to Laurier about Tony, he shrugged in his patented Gallic manner but agreed to a meeting. I offered to make dinner. Laurier had been a historian teaching at McGill when he decided to audition for CBC's *This*

Hour Has Seven Days. The program was a huge success. Canadians watched this Sunday night talk show in huge numbers and discussed it the next morning in a way that has rarely, if ever, attracted national attention before or since. Laurier was an enormous factor in its success with his outrageously confrontational style of questioning mitigated by his impish humour and Gallic charm. He and his co-hosts Patrick Watson and Dinah Christie had a symbiotic rapport that drove the show along as they interviewed some of the most prominent people in the country and tackled many of the major controversies of the day. Unaccountably, the CBC cancelled the show after only one season. It was said that the senior management thought the show too popular for a public broadcaster whose mandate was to treat events seriously. Or perhaps they were jealous of the instant popularity of the trio.

I had met Laurier when he became engaged to my friend Jo Armstrong. She was an upper-class young woman, a granddaughter of Edward Blake, an early leader of the federal Liberal party. Laurier was, in his own words, "a poor little habitant boy from la Beauce" whose parents were so impoverished that they handed him over to the Roman Catholic Church to bring up. He proved to be bright and his mentors steered him towards the priesthood. But he leaped over the wall, studied history, and after his marriage held a teaching position at McGill. He thoroughly enjoyed his newfound television celebrity, but at the same time his marriage was in trouble. Jo became aware that he was interested in young men. The couple went into counselling, but eventually Jo opted for divorce. Her mother told her, "My dear, in this family we don't divorce," to which Jo replied, "But Mother, Laurier is a homosexual."

When *This Hours Has Seven Days* was not renewed, the producer, Darryl Duke, offered Laurier his own interview show in Vancouver. Encouraged by his then-lover Chris Price, Laurier decided to make a whole new life for himself on the west coast. He settled into Vancouver happily enough, quickly made friends, set up housekeeping with an entourage comprising a number of gay cohorts, and entertained a wide acquaintance and was in turn entertained by them. He was a very social being and flourished in this new environment.

On the appointed day of the dinner with Tony, I went to the market and got a nice piece of fresh tuna, which I baked with fennel and mushrooms, followed by an apricot and crème fraîche dessert. Laurier was impressed by my culinary skills but less impressed by Tony, who was out of his element and unusually tongue-tied. I was used to his bubbly babble but unable to get him to open up. I could see that nothing much was going to come of this encounter and indeed nothing did.

A few days later I went to visit one of my former students, Mark Diamond, who was running the drama program at Simon Fraser University. When I knew Mark as a student, he was living with a very handsome young woman, Arlene Perly, who would later marry Bob Rae, the politician. Mark now had a new lady friend who taught with him in his program. Mark showed me around his studio and introduced me to one of his classes. He suggested that I might like to give a master class, and I obliged with a vocal class I had taught a good many times before based on ideas I had absorbed from the composer R. Murray Schafer. The class went well and afterwards I met Mark's technical director, who turned out to be the husband of Jennifer Mascall, the daughter of my actress friend Betty with whom I had worked in Toronto, and who gave me my first chance as a theatre director before her untimely death some years ago. I was invited to their house for dinner two nights later.

Mark strongly advised me to stay on in the evening to see a performance by a Quebec group, which he said was doing, frankly, the most imaginative work in the country. This seemed unlikely to me, but I agreed to remain on campus. The company presented a series of clever short pieces that combined mime, dance, and the spoken word. One piece I particularly remember involved a man and a woman who meet casually, become interested, circle each other tentatively, and, as they become infatuated, finally embrace, at which point their heads fall off. The company was Carbone 14 and its leader was Gilles Maheu. I would continue to follow their work in the next decade, and indeed they proved to be one of the most original troupes I have ever encountered.

My dinner with Jennifer Mascall was an extremely pleasant reunion. She had three young boys who were bright and extremely mannerly. I was charmed by them, and I told Jennifer I was certain her mother would have been extremely proud of her.

I learned that Jennifer was still dancing and, in fact, I attended a concert she gave a few evenings later. Her work seemed to me highly original. She was both lithe and graceful, a sort of elusive sprite. Her long red hair swept and swirled around her as she twisted and turned. Although it seemed to me that the theatre scene in Vancouver was rather more limited than in Toronto,

I found that modern dance was burgeoning there, an impression reinforced when I revisited the west coast some years later.

On an afternoon soon after that, Tony took me to see the Japanese gardens on the UBC campus. He seemed unfazed by his rather unsuccessful encounter with Laurier. "My dear Caligula, television is not really my thing, you know. My genius is poetic. One day I shall be deservedly recognized."

I returned to find the house empty except for young Kevin, who sat mournfully watching the television.

"How about a beer?"

"Why not? I need something to cheer me up."

"Still pining for your ex?"

"I thought I'd get over it and move on. He phoned this afternoon to say he misses me."

"Why don't you get back together?"

"He's married. He's Vietnamese and his family guilted him into it. And now he's going to be a father."

"You need to get laid."

"You're right. I suppose I could go to the Fruit Loop. Would you come with me?"

"Sure."

The Fruit Loop was an oval at the dead end of a street where male prostitutes hung out after dark. We set out on foot. The air was bracing and we moved along smartly. Two or three shadowy figures were standing about, their cigarettes glowing in the dark. We split up and I could see that before very long Kevin had connected with someone. They stood chatting for a minute and then took off down the street. I turned to go and was confronted by a young native boy.

"You ain't leavin'?"

"I think so."

"Can I come with you?"

"How old are you?'

"Eighteen."

"I don't believe you."

"You don't like young guys?'

"Sure but . . . anyway I've got no place to take you."

"We could go to the baths."

"I don't know where they are."

"I do." He took my hand and began to drag me along. I didn't really resist. The baths turned out to be only a few blocks away. We mounted to the second floor and the cashier gave the kid a knowing look. I paid for a room and a locker, the standard deal. We were admitted and went to our room.

"Let's walk around a bit, first. I'll show you the set-up." We went down a corridor, past the sauna to the hot tub. Sitting in it like a porpoise was Arthur. He greeted me cheerfully.

"I knew I'd see you here sooner or later. I see you're with Billy. My nephew. He's a nice boy. Very sweet and gentle. Be good to him."

We went back to our cubicle. Billy moved in and undressed me. Then he undressed himself. He was thin and delicate, with broad shoulders and a slim waist. He had a slight belly, a last bit of puppy fat. He lay down beside me and we snuggled together. Arthur was right; he was sweet and gentle. We kissed and held each other.

"You want to fuck me?"

"Not necessarily."

"You can if you want to."

"Let's just see how it goes."

We rubbed up against each other. We both came before we went to sleep. In the morning when I woke up, Billy was gone. I checked the pockets of my pants. I had deliberately left my wallet at home and only taken about fifty bucks with me. Billy had taken two bills and left me with a ten. Enough to get a cab back to the house.

I took Laurier and Chris to dinner and we went afterwards to hear June Katz sing. She was in good form and gave a selection of standards before coming to our table. "Hey, stranger," she greeted me. "I thought I'd be hearing from you. You'd better come and have lunch with me tomorrow. I'm not much of a cook, so curb your expectations."

"I'll bring a bottle of wine."

"Excellent."

Chris had wandered away to talk to some young male acquaintance, and Laurier was watching him closely.

"He's got a roving eye, that guy," June commented.

"Don't I know it."

A tall young man came over to our table. It took me a moment to recognize

David Sutherland, a former student and son of our neighbours in Rosedale. He was sporting a formidable moustache and his hair was much shorter than when he was a teenager. He greeted me enthusiastically and asked about Judy.

"She's teaching, so she couldn't come with me. What are you up to?" I asked.

"I finished my law degree. I'm with a small firm doing litigation. I think I may specialize in libel cases."

"Is there much call for that?"

"More all the time. Come over to our table. I want you to meet my partner."

He led me across the room and introduced me to a young woman who was in the last stages of pregnancy. "She's due in a few days. This is our last evening out, probably for quite a while."

"I'm resigned to breastfeeding and diapers but I'm not giving up my day job," she said.

"What's your day job?"

"I write for *Maclean's* about events on the coast."

"She's a got a pretty sharp eye," said David.

"All the better to keep track of you. He's a bit of a Casanova," she said. I knew that David had had a good many ladies. "I'm on to him. I know I can't change him, but maybe I can slow him down."

"You know I'll always be true to you, babe."

"In your fashion, as the lady says in the song."

They bantered back and forth a bit before excusing themselves, explaining that they felt they should get a good night's rest while they still could.

I went back to Laurier's table. He informed me that Chris had gone off with his young friend. We stayed till the end of June's next set and then I drove back to the house. Although it was Laurier's car, he didn't like to drive. He had given me a set of keys when I first arrived. Kevin informed me that Melissa had called and left me a message.

It was too late to call her back but I managed to get through to her the next morning. She told me that the cruise she had mentioned earlier was leaving in two days. She didn't know whether there would be room for me, but I could call the man who was organizing it. His name was George Butterfield.

"I know George. He's a good friend of my brother Bill." She gave me a number and I called George, who greeted me enthusiastically. It turned out that Bill and his wife Dorothy were also going on the cruise. George explained that this was a trial run. He had found a small steamship that could sleep about thirty passengers. George ran a very upscale travel agency. If this expedition was a success, he envisioned using the ship to organize cruises in the Mediterranean, the Caribbean, even Indonesia and the islands off Vietnam. Because it was an experiment, he was only charging the passengers one thousand dollars apiece, meals and drinks included. I could have a small cabin to myself. I signed on immediately and was given instructions where to meet the ship in two days' time.

My lunch with June consisted of chicken salad and a good deal of gossip. Emmanuelle's old Mercedes had broken down and June had advised her to ask her rich boyfriend for a new one: "You owe it to yourself, kid, and it's one way to find out if he's really serious." She then proceeded to analyze Laurier's relationship with Chris. "I think Laurier was smitten with Chris because he's good-looking and glamorous."

"He does come from a prominent Anglo family in Quebec. As a poor little habitant boy, as he likes to call himself, Laurier would be impressed by that."

"It fits. But Chris is losing interest. I can tell. Fortunately for Laurier, he's landed a good job. I have a lot of gay friends. I've watched this scene over and over. The number of gay relationships that last even a couple of years is tiny. I'm saying this because I sense you're flirting with joining the gay world. Watch your step, is my advice."

"You divorced your husband."

"We separated. We're still close. We talk regularly about our boys. We even go out on a date occasionally."

"But you have a boyfriend."

"He's a sweet guy but it's not serious. He knows that. I needed some space, that's all."

"I guess I did too."

"So you've got it. But be careful about what you throw away. How long do you expect to stay in Vancouver?"

"I haven't set myself a time limit. I'm going on a cruise up the channel day after tomorrow."

"You should set yourself a time limit after you get back. I'm serious."

Two days later I went to the docks in mid-afternoon. George was waiting for me with a friendly grin. I was shown to my cabin, which brought back memories of my first crossing of the Atlantic in the mid-'50s and my time as a cadet on board a destroyer. I stowed my limited gear, reverting to the naval terminology I vaguely remembered, went up on deck and watched while the crew cast off. Several other passengers introduced themselves. Besides Bill and Dorothy, there was a couple that I knew from Toronto. Most of the others were Americans. We started to move through the calm waters of the channel. George assembled us for cocktails at about four-thirty. Introductions all round. It seemed like a friendly and genial group. Jeremy, a young photographer, was part of the group. His job was to make a record of the trip. He was extremely agile and kept climbing up onto the forecastle or lying down on the deck to shoot from a variety of angles.

The dinner was excellent: a fish soup followed by boeuf en daube and gateau St. Honoré. It was accompanied by excellent French wines: Veuve Clicquot, Chablis, Pommard. George had imported a French chef for this expedition. He had made a specialty of bicycle tours of rural France. His clients cycled from one hostellerie or chateau to another; their baggage was driven separately so that it would be awaiting them when they arrived. One of his children would marry into a French family that owned vineyards in the Burgundy region, and eventually George and his wife Martha would acquire a flat in the walls of the city of Beaune in Burgundy.

There was a French couple on the tour. After dinner they wanted to have a couple of rubbers of bridge. The woman's mother would join them but they needed a third. Reluctantly, I agreed to make up a fourth. My father, who was a crack bridge player, had tried to teach me the game. Invariably, after a hand or two, I would commit some stupid error and he would be in a rage. Unlike my father-in-law, also an excellent bridge player, he did not scream and shout, but regarded me with cold contempt. I had given up and had not played for some years. But I figured I could give them a passable game, and I could follow their French fairly well.

I knew that serious bridge players concentrated on their cards in silence, but these people talked incessantly and often decided to go back and replay another card. They were vivacious and obviously enjoying themselves. I soon began to share their enjoyment. I would play with them several evenings during the cruise.

Breakfast was allowed to extend over most of the morning. Some of the passengers got up early; other rarely appeared till noon. Some of the passengers were ready to start drinking as soon as the bar opened at eleven in the morning. Melissa and Jake, the other graduate student, gave lectures on the culture of the west coast tribes. We learned about their winter ceremonies, the identification of their various clans with certain specific animals (raven, bear, snake, and owl), the role of the shamans in consulting their ancestors, their tradition of placing the corpses of their dead in trees.

The second day, we visited a native reserve. The people were welcoming. They had prepared a feast for us: baked salmon and some sort of vegetables. It smelled delicious but tasted disgusting. However, we bravely downed it so as not to offend our hosts. We hoped they might dance for us but were told the dances were strictly a winter phenomenon and, in any case, they were wary of sharing their secrets with white men.

The next day we slowed down to pass an abandoned native village. Tall, weathered totem poles stood near the shore against a background of towering conifers. There was a desire on the part of some of our party to go swimming. I decided to join them. The water was freezing cold but we made our way to the shore and stood looking up at the totems. We amused ourselves by trying to identify the various creatures whose enigmatic faces looked down on us, impervious to our frivolous comments. Jake was able to correct some of our mistaken impressions. Back on board, Melissa joined me at the railing as we started to move on. "I thought you might visit me last night," she said with a challenging grin.

It was the time of the Falklands War. One American expressed his indignation that the British had the temerity to try to hold onto these tiny islands off the coast of Argentina. "Don't the fucking British know their empire is a thing of the past? I hope the Argentinos beat the pants off them and send them home in disgrace." This called forth a heated response from some of the Canadians. Two or three of them sang "Rule, Britannia!" with great gusto. George suggested that we all sing our native anthems and lit into "The Marseillaise," which the French passengers joined with enthusiasm. An Australian couple followed up with "Waltzing Matilda," and the animosity dissolved into a somewhat boozy haze of camaraderie.

Late in the evening, I made my way to Melissa's cabin and, finding the door unlocked, opened it to find Melissa in bed with Jake. "You could join us if you like." I thought about it for a moment and then retreated. I went back to my own cabin to find Jeremy in my bunk with the cabin boy. "I was pretty sure you wouldn't mind," Jeremy grinned at me.

"I'll leave you to it," I said. I went up on deck and stood listening to the waves lapping against the sides of the boat. Except for that, there was complete silence. The stars shone brightly above me in the night sky. I remembered being on night watch as a cadet, the feeling of awe at the immensity of the ocean and the quiet of the universe as the planets revolved in their orbits.

On the final night of the cruise we decided to hold our own potlatch. Early in the day we were provided with coloured paper from which we constructed masks, some of them quite ingenious. In the late afternoon we gathered, sporting our paper creations. Some of the men had stripped down to their underpants. The women wore their choicest cocktail gowns. Much hooch was consumed. A buffet supper featured salmon and corn on the cob.

Jeremy produced bongo drums, and some of the men danced in what they imagined was the manner of native warriors. There was a good deal of shouting and laughter. When I finally retired to my cabin I found Melissa waiting for me. We climbed into my bunk together, but because of my alcoholic consumption, I wasn't able to perform. The next day I had a crashing headache. I staggered ashore and headed for Laurier's house, where I went to bed and slept for the best part of twenty-four hours.

A few weeks later I received a letter from George. He asked me to send him an additional cheque for five hundred dollars to cover the cost of all the liquor and wine we had consumed. He also informed me that the captain of the little steamship had said that although he had quite enjoyed our cruise, he never wanted to repeat the experience.

I came down to dinner the next night to find Laurier sitting disconsolately in the living room with a glass of Scotch. "You look rather morose," I said. "What's the matter?"

"Chris has gone off to Whistler with that kid."

"It's probably just for a fling."

"I don't think so."

"You really love him?"

Laurier nodded.

"You'll find somebody else."

"I suppose so. That's my future, always chasing after someone I can't have."

"You may find Mr. Right."

"I should never have left Jo."

"Maybe you could go back to her."

"No, she has too much pride."

"I guess you're right."

"For that matter, so have I. You should go back to Judy before it's too late."

I decided to go for a long walk. I thought about Laurier's advice. I'd had fun in Vancouver but I hadn't uncovered any prospects of work. And I did want to work. I had some good contacts here in Vancouver, but it was clear to me that I would have to move here in order to develop them. Probably Judy would move with me if I asked her to, but she had a career as a teacher in Toronto, where she was known and highly respected. With her limited academic qualifications, it might be hard for her to have a similar position in Vancouver. Did I really want to be on my own? I had never lived alone for more than a few months in my whole life. I found the prospect daunting — frightening, even.

I walked along and, without consciously knowing it, I found myself heading towards the Fruit Loop. In the shadows, I saw Billy. He looked up and saw me and started to move rapidly away. I called out to him, and he stopped but didn't turn to look at me. I went over to him.

"You don't remember me?"

"I thought you'd be mad at me."

"Why? Because you took a few bills out of my wallet? You'd earned them."

"I got to live somehow."

"I know."

"You was very nice to me."

"You were very nice to me."

"You want to go to the tubs again?"

I thought for a minute. "No."

"Okay then."

"Give me a hug."

I felt his warm body pressed against mine. We stayed holding each other for maybe five minutes. I gave him twenty bucks and walked away.

The next day I had lunch with Tony.

"I'm going back to Toronto," I told him.

"I'm not surprised. Maybe I should go back to Toronto too. Look for work."

"I don't think so. You've settled in here. This place suits you. And work doesn't. Anyway, your mother depends on you."

Tony sighed. “Death by the sea.”

We went for a walk along the seawall surrounding Stanley Park. The sun was shining and the sea was calm. We looked out across it at the mountains and then turned back. The dark forest beckoned. “It’s so beautiful here,” I said.

“I think I’ll just see who’s out cruising this afternoon.”

“Keep in touch,” I said.

Tony headed into the woods. I stood and watched until he disappeared. The next day I got on a plane and flew back to Toronto.

JOHNNY BANANAS

I fell in love with Italy even before I went there, through the pictures in the *Books of Knowledge* in my parents' library. Michelangelo's *David*, the Piazza San Marco, the Coliseum, and Botticelli's *Primavera* were indelibly stamped in my brain long before I saw them during our visit to Italy with the kids in 1971. I returned to work at the university determined to learn the language. I discovered I could attend a class every morning at nine o'clock taught by a woman who was a fluent speaker. Although we did learn some grammar, the class was primarily conversational. The students were Italian-Canadians who either wanted a "bird" course or wished to improve their command of standard Italian, as most of them spoke dialects at home.

After two years, I had achieved a working command of the language and was determined to put it to the test. At the end of term I flew to Rome and looked up my friend Gilbert Reid in an old palazzo just off Via Condotti, where he held forth as cultural attaché to the Canadian Embassy. Every Canadian of any note who went to Rome passed through Gilbert's hands, from Robertson Davies to Adrienne Clarkson, and he was on intimate terms with the Canadian contingent living in Rome, ranging from the photographer Roloff Beny to the socialite Sandra Labatt, who had married an Italian banker and lived a very stylish life consorting with contessas and principessas. We went to cocktail parties and enjoyed dinners at Gilbert's favourite trattorias in piazzas where fountains splashed and strolling musicians serenaded us under the stars.

After a week I decided to rent a farmhouse belonging to Gilbert's assistant Elena Solari on the outskirts of Orvieto, halfway between Rome and Florence. The old walled city sits on top of a hill and has not changed appreciably since the fifteenth century, when the cathedral was completed, its façade resplendent with black and white marble and carvings of biblical scenes, its interior chapels decorated with apocalyptic frescoes of the *Last Judgment* by Luca Signorelli. I walked the streets by day and dined at the many excellent restaurants by night. One of these was the tiny Trattoria dell'Orso, whose chef and owner was Gabriele, a short jolly man and a wonderful cook. Occasionally his mother helped him and his boyfriend, Ciro, in the kitchen and I was soon taking language lessons from his sister Rita. About the third time I had dinner at the Orso I was surprised to find how low my bill was. When I challenged Gabriele, he smiled and said, "*Prezzo d'amico.*"

From then on, I ate at Gabriele's almost every evening and soon met other expatriates who lived in the city or nearby. There was a retired American doctor and his second wife, who had bought a rather decayed palazzo and were busy restoring it.

Every week they gave a reception for a few friends in their salotto, which was decorated with undistinguished but original fifteenth-century frescoes. We drank the crisp white wine of Orvieto while our hostess played the harp, and the talk ranged from the quality of antiques dealers in a nearby town, most of whom were said to be thieves, to Italian politics, which were treated by these chic foreigners with amused contempt. Neither the Italian Communists nor the neo-Fascists were to be taken seriously.

I had rented a little car on expeditions to see such local curiosities as the park of Bomarzo with its huge stone monsters and the Villa Lante with its fountains that could be activated by a secret foot pedal, a device invented by its original owner, a mischievous cardinal who delighted in giving his guests a sudden, unexpected soaking. Another time, I drove to the sea and walked along the beach. Uncertain of whom I might meet, I had locked my wallet in the car. I returned to find the car had been broken into, my wallet stolen, and for good measure the thief had flatted all my tires. It was almost impossible to steer but I made my way slowly to the nearest garage. The mechanics were amused but said I would have to leave the car with them overnight. I called Gabriele who left the supervision of his kitchen to his mother and came and picked me up.

The next day he drove me back to the garage, where I recovered my car. Gabriele insisted that the cost of the new tires should be covered by insurance. He got on the phone and negotiated with the rental company until he had convinced them. I had also lost my credit cards, and Gabriele phoned American Express and convinced them to deliver a new card to my farmhouse the next day. Gabriele informed me that the thieves had already racked up purchases to the tune of thirty thousand dollars at a jewellery store. Fortunately, I had phoned to report the loss of my card from the garage the day before and so I was not liable for these charges. Gabriele explained that the thieves had not actually bought the jewellery; they had a deal with the jeweller, and if they got away with their scam they would split the profits. "*Dunque, mi amico,* you are enjoy the full Italian experience."

I returned to my job as director of Hart House Theatre determined to return to Italy on my next vacation, little imagining that my next encounter with Italian culture would happen in Toronto. I was auditioning actors for a production of Shakespeare's *Troilus and Cressida,* a play with a very large cast. By the end of a week of seeing aspiring actors, I felt I had the makings of a good cast, although I was still missing a few key characters. At five o'clock on a Friday afternoon, two rather short young men appeared together on the stage. Damiano Pietropaolo did not give a very impressive audition but was obviously highly intelligent. He became my assistant director on the production and went on to direct several productions at the Drama Centre. His companion, Michael Macina, was immediately recognizable as a gifted actor. He had the edgy, nervous quality I had been hoping to find in someone to play the cynical Thersites. Both would become good friends.

Michael's performance in that role was bold and outrageous. He created a sort of distorted mirror image of the scheming Ulysses of Rod Beattie. These two actors gave weight and depth to this tale of doomed love and inflated heroism. They both attracted the attention of critics and directors, which would propel them along creative paths they would pursue for the rest of their lives.

The following year, the committee of academics who selected the works to be produced at Hart House Theatre decreed that I should direct something by Aristophanes. I rejected *Lysistrata* as a one-joke play and instead decided to adapt *The Frogs,* a play which satirizes the work of various Athenian dramatists. I decided no one would get the ancient jokes and allusions, so I completely rewrote the text and set it in modern times, though following the structure of the original. The central characters are Hercules, Dionysus, and Xanthius, a slave. These I recast as a jock, a gay, and a lovesick girl. Instead of parodies of Greek plays we introduced send-ups of Michael Ondaatje's *The Collected Works of Billy the Kid,* Michel Tremblay's *Hosanna,* and David French's Newfoundland plays, then the hits of the Toronto alternative theatre scene. There were recurring scatological jokes and songs that parodied such standard tunes as "Begin the Beguine" and "Over the Rainbow."

Michael Macina, though short of stature, was a beautiful young man and he proved a dashing partner for Barbara Stewart, who played the frustrated young woman in their romantic encounters. He also proved a natural comic, and his impersonations of Richard Monette as Hosanna, Nick Mancuso as Billy the Kid, and Pierre Trudeau were accurate and hilarious. The show was panned by critics and academics alike, but the student audience seemed to enjoy it.

That summer Michael worked with me as an instructor in my Youtheatre workshops. He was popular with the kids, especially the young women, and I began to realize that Michael, undeterred by his stature, was an enthusiastic womanizer. He decided not to continue his academic studies and I lost touch with him for a few years, though I heard that he had become very involved with avant-garde theatre in Paris and Montreal. He read Artaud and Brecht and became a disciple of Grotowski, all the fashionable dramatic theorists of the day.

One day he called me and suggested we have lunch. We quickly demolished a bottle of Chianti before he told me that he had written a play about his grandfather, who had operated a fruit stand — or, in what was known in Toronto's Little Italy as Italese, *fruttistenda* — on Bay Street in the '20s. I read it and was surprised that it showed little or no evidence of the influence of the critics and practitioners whose ideas he had been so keen to absorb. It was an episodic, realistic chronicle of the ups and downs of a family spanning some forty years. I thought it had real possibilities if he was prepared to do some cutting and reworking to strengthen the storyline from the arrival of immigrants in Toronto early in the twentieth century to their gradual assimilation into their adopted city. I agreed to work on the script with Michael and to direct a production of the play — and so began my career as a theatrical producer.

The play, *Johnny Bananas*, is set in "The Ward," the section of Toronto bound by Bay, Spadina, King, and Dundas. It was a part of the city I knew intimately as I walked its streets every summer for four years working as a messenger boy delivering paper samples to the many printers in the area. That was in the '40s and the old houses and office buildings had changed little since the beginning of the last century. There were gypsy fortune tellers on Queen Street, peddlers drove horse-drawn carts collecting junk, Orthodox Jews with beards and prayer shawls walked home with live chickens bought from the neighbourhood shochet, and across from our warehouse there was a steam bath which was actually a brothel; on a warm day the whores would sometimes sit in the windows, waiting for some truck driver to pay them a visit on his lunch hour.

I wanted to catch some of this remembered atmosphere in my production, and my actors responded to my stories by coming up with inventive detail. Michael's language had a raw, idiosyncratic energy that came partly from the characters' attempts to express themselves in their newly acquired language. I wanted the short scenes to flow into one another. There was no set, just a few pieces of furniture and a hand-drawn cart that Reed Needles built for us. We improvised street scenes as we worked on the piece but the finished script remained very much Michael's creation.

It was obvious to me that Michael should play the protagonist, Johnny, himself. The opening scenes, in which there was a lot of Italian, were initially problematic. Michael had become fluent in French but as a third-generation Canadian he had little or no Italian. I called in Damiano, who was born in Calabria and was familiar with not only the elegant Tuscan of the well-educated, but also the southern dialect that these people would have spoken. Damiano corrected Michael's dialogue and also coached him until he was satisfied with his pronunciation and use of distinctive Italian gestures.

I decided that the cast should be made up entirely of actors with an Italian background. They wouldn't have to be concerned with acting Italian; they would *be* Italian. I cast Damiano as Johnny's father and his wife, Mariella, as his mother. Damiano brought in his friend Celestino and his son Paolo. He also found us Tonia Serrao, a warm and sympathetic actress who played Johnny's long-suffering wife. We found two beautiful young actors, Darlene Mignacco and Frank Pellegrino, to round out the family. The only member who was not of Italian decent was Angelo Rizacos, whose family was Greek but who proved a quick study and picked up the lingo rapidly.

There was one Anglo character in the script, a politician who befriended Johnny. This role was played by Rod Beattie, who was on hiatus from the Stratford company. One night during rehearsal, I was surprised to see a woman sitting quietly at the back of the room. It was Martha Henry. I soon learned that Rod Beattie was courting her. Their relationship blossomed and before long led to marriage.

It was a very amiable company. I had worked with about half of the actors before and they accepted my direction without serious reservations. I occasionally gave them instructions in Italian and they were tolerant of this little show of vanity on my part. In one scene, young Paolo, who was about eleven years old, was supposed to get in bed with one of the actresses. He refused to do this. I recall Rod Beattie saying to him, "Young man, the day will come when you will regret not taking advantage of this opportunity." We rehearsed mostly in the evenings, as most of my actors worked during the day. After about six weeks, we were ready to put the show in front of an audience.

On opening night, the actors assembled. At fifteen minutes before the curtain was to go up the stage manager came to me in a panic. Where was Michael? She had phoned his house and received no answer. I then phoned his mother who had no idea where he was. What could we do? Could I go on in his place?

In fact, I knew the script fairly well. At that stage of my life I had a pretty good memory. Indeed, I had once gone on in place of David Gardner as Lopakhin in *The Cherry Orchard* when he cut his big toe off with an electric lawnmower. Of course I couldn't fit into Michael's costume, although I could probably wear his battered fedora. I was sitting in a dressing room trying to psych myself up for the ordeal ahead at about three minutes to curtain when Michael walked in. He was completely unapologetic. He had decided he needed a nap before the show. It had not occurred to him that he might have let the stage manager know. I couldn't help suspecting that Michael had planned the whole thing as an attention-getting device. I knew by now that there was a perverse streak in his nature. He gave a splendid performance that night: caustic, arrogant and ultimately pathetic. A performance rooted in his own complex and stubborn character.

The play attracted an enthusiastic public not entirely composed of Italian-Canadians, though they formed a substantial part of our audience, and word of mouth was an important factor in our success, as we had virtually no advertising budget. At the end of the run we were invited to do several performances at the Centro Colombo, the spacious and elegant Italian club on St. Clair Avenue West. We had a brief down period and then remounted the play at the old Courthouse Theatre on Adelaide Street. At the end of the run I realized I had lost about ten thousand dollars on the production. Michael vowed to repay me or at least split the loss. I didn't imagine he would be able to do this, and of course it didn't happen.

The year before, I had gone to visit friends in Vancouver. While there I saw a performance of *The Dresser* with William Hutt and Robin Phillips. Bill was an old friend, having directed me as an undergraduate. Robin I had met when he was directing his company at the Grand Theatre in London, Ontario. Rod Beattie had given him a play I had written and he was considering producing it in his second season. But there wasn't a second season. After the performance of *The Dresser*, I went backstage and greeted Bill. I suggested we might go for a drink. Bill gave me a wry smile and said, "Let's have lunch tomorrow. Robin's waiting for you in his dressing room."

I knocked on the door and a voice asked me to go in. Robin was sitting, ostensibly removing his makeup. He was naked except for a very brief pair of briefs. He gave me a smile and we sat in silence for a moment. Robin was still young and handsome, and he had a very good body. I wondered if he was waiting for me to make the first move.

I thought about it for a minute and decided it would be a mistake to have a sexual liaison with Robin, however short-lived. Just as I had never been sexually involved with any of my students, I thought it foolish to take up with actors. I suggested we go for a drink and we did.

Robin and I stayed in touch after we both came back east and we met once or twice for dinner. He expressed an interest in seeing *Johnny Bananas*. I took him to see a performance and he was quite complimentary about the script, the direction, and some of the acting. He left after the intermission, which did not trouble me. I knew this was his usual custom. The word had got around backstage that Robin was in the audience, and the actors were disappointed that he did not stay to the end. Robin was still a name to conjure with and they must have hoped he might advance their careers. But by this time Robin no longer had a theatre of his own.

At the end of the run, as was my custom, we gave a cast party at our house on Sherbourne Street. Judy made one of her delicious casseroles and herbed bread. I made a salad and stocked up on Italian cheeses at the market: burrata, caprino, parmigiano-reggiano, pecorino, mozzarella di bufala, gorgonzola, and torta di mascarpone. There was much gossip and laughter as the cast sat on the floor in the living room in front of a roaring fire. Darlene presented me with several bottles of wine made by the families of cast members and said, "Martin, we've decided to make you an honorary Italian."

I thought this would be the end of *Johnny Bananas* but I was wrong. A few years later, Damiano, now a CBC Radio producer, decided that the play could be adapted for radio. Michael and I worked on the script, recasting it into five fifteen-minute episodes to be broadcast on *Morningside*, the popular radio show hosted by Peter Gzowski. Tony Nardi played Johnny and R. H. Thomson took over the role originated by Rod Beattie. The play reached a much wider audience across the country and elicited favourable comments from the listening public.

Damiano asked Michael and I to sit with him in the control booth and we did. I watched with interest and picked up some useful clues about producing radio. Michael, however, looked haggard and preoccupied and fell asleep several times during the recording session. Afterwards Damiano said to me, "I hoped that both you and Michael would learn something. You made some good comments and suggestions but I don't think Michael got much out of it. Too bad, he needs the work. I worry about him."

Some months later, Michael phoned me and told me he was getting married. He asked me to be his best man. I was completely taken by surprise but quickly agreed. I met his bride-to-be, Dorothy, a blonde airline stewardess half a head taller than Michael. I liked her; she was stylish and intelligent, and I was happy to think that Michael was settling down and would have someone to help him pull together his talents and reshape his scattered life.

The wedding was non-religious, though I knew Michael had attended a Catholic boys' school. Michael and I wore white dinner jackets, and the bride wore black, all quite deliberately unconventional. Both Michael and I made speeches, he mainly in French. Dorothy, as a stewardess, was fluent in French and no doubt this was part of her appeal to Michael. A good deal of champagne was consumed and the party went on until about three in the morning. Looking around the apartment where Michael and Dorothy were to set up housekeeping, I realized many of the guests were Michael's former girlfriends. I'm sure they wished him well, for Michael, though strong-willed to the point of contrariness, had a good heart. But the marriage didn't last long. I and other friends who visited them soon learned that Michael and Dorothy fought almost continuously when she was there, and when she wasn't, Michael was drinking heavily.

Michael and I continued to have lunch every month or two. He had begun working with a small computer company. He had also met a producer who encouraged him to adapt *Johnny Bananas* for television.

Michael and I set to work and produced an outline and scripts for three half-hour episodes. We shopped them to the CBC without success. The timing was wrong; Canadian television was not yet ready for multiculturalism. We eventually realized our project was not going anywhere.

I saw less of Michael but we still occasionally met for lunch. Michael had lost his looks. His face was patchy. He was bald with a great fringe of long hair at the sides. He looked eccentric and a bit ridiculous. I learned he was living with a woman. When he suggested I might like to meet her, I readily agreed. We met in a bar one afternoon. They were both drunk and quarrelsome. I decided that our lunches, which always involved at least one bottle of wine, were probably not a good idea.

The next time we met for lunch, Michael was accompanied by his four-year-old daughter. She was a pretty little thing with a good deal of mischievous charm and entered into the conversation without hesitation. Michael told me that he had split up with her mother and that the daughter was living mainly with him. He limited himself to two glasses of wine and confessed that his doctor was concerned about the state of his liver. His face had a yellowish cast and his hair was almost white. He looked about seventy years old, although I knew he must only be in his early fifties.

We spent most of the afternoon together. He was his usual garrulous self, making not-very-funny jokes at which he laughed mirthlessly, uttering pronouncements about art and politics, running off on tangents. I was reminded how difficult it had always been to get him to stick to the subject, to centre down on whatever we were working on. He had always been full of ideas, many of which were impractical or irrelevant or both. His mind was like a butterfly, flitting from topic to topic, never settling anywhere. It was part of his charm and at the same time infuriating.

Some months later I was at the cottage when I received an email telling me Michael had died. I wondered what had happened to his daughter. I phoned his mother and learned she was looking after the girl. Apparently Michael had been looking for a donor so that he could have a liver transplant, but no one had offered to help him. Mrs. Macina said that some friends were planning a memorial for Michael, and I asked her to tell them to get in touch with me. But I heard no more. At least Michael had achieved one of his dreams: he wrote a play with a perfect role for himself and played it to the hilt.

MOVIE MADNESS

When I left the Drama Centre my former boss-lady, Ann Saddlemyer, asked me, "What are you going to do now?"

"I'm going to make movies," I replied confidently.

The last year I taught my theatre course at the university, there was a kid in the class who looked rather like a young Robert Redford. His name was Kevin Sullivan. He proved to be not only handsome but bright. He did an assignment that involved splicing together spoken words, music, and sound effects that was like the work of an accomplished professional editor. He auditioned for me and played a leading role in my production of *Women of Trachis*. In November he came to me and said, "I want to make a movie. And I want you to direct it."

I was flattered. We worked together on a script adapted from Hans Christian Andersen's "The Fir Tree." It centred on a family Christmas in a late nineteenth-century farmhouse. We cast it with student actors Katie Knox and Nic Labriola, as well as my wife, Judy, and John Gilbert, a professor of French literature at the university, as the parents. Kevin was to play the love interest of the oldest daughter. Martha Mann agreed to assemble the period costumes. Kevin went to Black Creek Pioneer Village, which was closed for the winter season, and talked the manager into letting us shoot there as soon as there was any snow. The manager even agreed to let us use their sleigh and team of horses. Kevin would drive the sleigh. He had never done it before but this didn't faze him.

Kevin found a capable photographer with a good movie camera. His mother agreed to provide food for the actors. There was no snow until after Christmas that year, but as soon as it covered the ground, Mrs. Sullivan toured the neighbourhood in her car and found a discarded Christmas tree. She decorated it with her own ornaments, under Kevin's supervision. We all went up to Pioneer Village and, standing behind the cameraman, I ordered the actors about. Kevin, when he was not on camera, stood beside me and made suggestions, most of which were superior to my ideas. We were all chilled to the bone but cheered on by Mrs. Sullivan's hot chocolate and homemade doughnuts.

We finished the shoot at the village in four days and followed up with another brief shoot in the Rosedale Ravine for a snowball fight when Kevin was not satisfied with the original take. Kevin then went into the editing room at the university's film centre on St. George Street and cut the various scenes together. He persuaded a friend to write music for the soundtrack and laid it in. The finished result was a half-hour film of great charm and warmth. The cost had been about seven thousand dollars, mostly for stock and processing.

Kevin took *The Fir Tree* to the CBC, who agreed to broadcast it as a holiday special. They paid him five thousand dollars for the initial showing. He was shrewd enough to hang onto the rights for future broadcast, and the film was aired every Christmas for the next four or five years. I was well aware that the whole enterprise was the result of Kevin's initiative, energy, and ability to charm people into doing things for him. But it encouraged me to think that maybe I could find a place in the world of film.

It was an art that had long fascinated me. My very first movie was *Snow White*. I must have been about five when my father took me to see it, and I recall he was impressed that I was not scared of the witch, but I don't remember that he took me to many more movies. Kay Williams, my friend Dick's mother, took us to see all the early Disney movies: *Pinocchio*, *Dumbo*, and *Fantasia*, as well as *The Thief of Bagdad* and *Up in Arms*, which introduced us to Danny Kaye. Soon Dick and I were going to the local movie house almost every Saturday afternoon. We saw newsreels because it was wartime; serials of *Tarzan* and *The Lone Ranger*; the *Road* movies featuring Bob Hope, Bing Crosby, and Dorothy Lamour; Dagwood and Blondie movies; and our favourites, The Marx Brothers in *A Night at the Opera*, and Olsen and Johnson in *Hellzapoppin'*.

These outings I financed with my allowance, which initially was a quarter a week. I was instructed to spend ten cents of this on collection every week at Sunday school and ten cents every other week on a haircut. The rest was mine to do with as I wished. I preferred movies to buying candy and, anyway, Mother made excellent maple fudge.

Even after I started to act in plays, movies seemed to me a superior art form. I liked historical movies, beginning with *Gone with the Wind* and *The Scarlet Pimpernel*. I zoned in on the British movies that started to be shown at the Odeon cinemas after the war. Alastair Sim and Alec Guinness replaced James Cagney and Cary Grant as my favourite actors. Then there were the theatrical spectacles of Michael Powell and Emeric Pressburger, *The Red Shoes* and *The Tales of Hoffman*. And from France, *Les Enfants du Paradis*. I continued to go to Disney's movies as they appeared but, except for *The Jungle Book*, they didn't seem to have the same magic as his first films. While I was still a teenager, some of Charlie Chaplin's early movies were re-released: *The Gold Rush, Modern Times*, and *The Great Dictator*.

These were the motion pictures that stimulated my imagination as I was growing up. I would continue to go to movies for the rest of my life and would follow the careers of my favourite stars: Vivien Leigh, Ralph Richardson, Marlon Brando, Warren Beatty, Julie Christie, Laurence Olivier, Marilyn Monroe, Maggie Smith, Judi Dench, and Peter O'Toole. Led on by Pauline Kael, my enthusiasm would embrace the *nouvelle vague* and the American independents. As I was now working as a stage director, I began to identify with film directors: Jean-Luc Godard, François Truffaut, Louis Malle, Federico Fellini, Mike Nichols, Billy Wilder, John Huston, Alfred Hitchcock, and later Stephen Frears and Mike Leigh. It was undoubtedly presumptuous of me, but I decided to aim high. In high school one of my teachers introduced me to Browning and I remembered his line, "a man's reach should exceed his grasp." It was a motto I took to heart.

Of course, if I had been serious about working in the movies, I should have done what Dick had done and gone to Los Angeles as a teenager. Or stayed in London in the '50s when I had actually made some film connections. Or even stayed in London in the early '80s after I left the university. There has never been much of a movie industry in Canada, except in Quebec, for the same reasons as there has never been much of a publishing industry. The potential audience, which in my childhood was colonized by the British, had become colonized by the Americans. I came to understand that the moguls of Hollywood were happy to have Canadians working in their films as long as they retained control of production and distribution. The only Canadian writers, performers, and directors who could make decent livings and reach a wide audience were the ones who were able sell their work in Britain or the United States.

I thought it might be different in television. In the 1980s the CBC was turning out a fair amount of original Canadian dramatic programming. I decided to produce a pilot for a sitcom. It was called *Roomers* and involved a group of people who shared a boarding house run by an eccentric older woman. I co-opted my long-time friend Juliana Saxton to play this role as a sort of aristocratic den-mother down on her luck. The roomers were mostly kids from my various drama classes. Kevin, Sheila Russell, and David Wilkinson were the regulars, and there would be various other visitors, including David's friend Lee, a very pretty drama student from Ryerson who specialized in makeup and whom he dubbed "Miss Fancyface." Bernard Leroux, a photography student at the art college, would shoot the piece. David worked on the script with me. He lived in a shared house on Carlton Street and we were able to persuade some of the other people living in the house to let us use it for the shoot. Robert Gage, a fashionable hairdresser for whom David did some part-time work, agreed to do the women's hair, and Fancyface did the makeup. I directed the shoot and turned the film over to Kevin to edit.

I thought the finished pilot was quite stylish and funny. My brother's friend Julian Porter had introduced me to Michael Levine, a young entertainment lawyer. I told him about the project and he seemed interested. He offered to show it to a senior CBC producer of his acquaintance. I gave him the tape and waited. Eventually, I called him and he reported that the producer had thought the tape was terrible. At the time, there really was no other network to send the print to. So we all moved on.

This would not be my last encounter with Michael Levine, who remained friendly. I knew that he had been influential in shaping the careers of Patrick Watson, Veronica Tennant, and Adrienne Clarkson, among others. However, every time I went to him with a project, though often he seemed confident that it had value, he proved unable to move it forward. I was forced to realize I was not in his league.

Shortly after this, Kevin came to me to work on the screenplay for a film about Cornelius Krieghoff, the Dutch painter who specialized in scenes of rural life in Quebec in the nineteenth century. Kevin had managed to persuade Ken Thomson to let him photograph the paintings in his extensive collection of Krieghoff paintings. We devised a rather sentimental scenario based on what we knew of Krieghoff's life story. I came to realize that Kevin had a natural affinity for stories that were somewhat melodramatic, warmhearted, and at the same time bittersweet. We differed on the ending of the screenplay. I also thought that some of the scenes should involve dialogue in French; after all, much of it took place in rural Quebec. Kevin proved rather stubborn in resisting my ideas and we agreed to part without rancour. I told him he could use whatever parts of my work he wished and, in fact, he did. I was still fully employed at the university and had more than enough to keep me busy. Had I realized that Kevin would become one of the most successful filmmakers in Canada, I might have given up my university job to work with him and thus realized my ambitions as a screenwriter and perhaps a director.

For all his charm, Kevin, when I knew him, was a bit of a scatterbrain. He was almost invariably late for appointments and rehearsals. He once arrived five minutes after the start of a performance. Fortunately his character did not appear in the first scene. Soon after we shot *The Fir Tree* he was dating an attractive and strong-minded young woman named Trudy Grant. I remember her saying to him, "Kevin, I know you and your friends think it's cute that you keep people waiting and usually turn up late, but I don't think it's cute. If you're going to be with me, you can smarten up and be responsible." Trudy and Kevin were married shortly after his graduation at St. Basil's Collegiate Church on campus with a lavish reception at the yacht club. Trudy came from a wealthy northern Ontario lumber family, and she not only invested family money in Kevin's fledgling production company, but became his business partner, managing the financial affairs with a tough and shrewd competence.

Kevin wrote a screenplay for a family western film and cast Marilyn Lightstone in the lead, thereby gaining access to Moses Znaimer's TV network for distribution. He then acquired the rights to film *Anne of Green Gables* from the estate of Lucy Maud Montgomery. The film starred Megan Follows and Jonathan Crombie, son of the former mayor and federal cabinet minister, and was a big financial success. It led to the TV series *Road to Avonlea*, also based on Montgomery's novels, which Kevin produced in association with the CBC and the Disney organization. It ran for seven seasons and was enormously popular, not only in Canada and the United States but around the world. It employed hundreds of Canadian actors and made stars of Sarah Polley, R. H. Thomson, and Jackie Burroughs.

Some people have denigrated Kevin because he could be tight-fisted and sometimes indulged in fits of temper. They thought his films were hypocritical, exploiting nineteenth-century sentimentality. But in fact Kevin's work was very much a product of his own sensibility. He believed in the wholesomeness of family life and old-fashioned morality. And he certainly understood what North American families of the day were looking for in the way of heart-warming entertainment. Once when I was in Italy, I was eating alone in a restaurant. There was an American family at the next table. They asked me what I did and I said I was a writer. They asked if I had ever worked on anything they might have heard of. I mentioned *Road to Avonlea* and their faces lit up. "You actually know Jackie Burroughs?" they gasped as they moved to my table. They had seen every episode.

Well into the fifth season of the show, I got a call from my friend Anne Tait. She had been a casting director at CBC working with Diane Polley. I knew Diane when she was an amateur actress for the Women's Alumnae. I remember when she told me she was pregnant for the fifth time: "I'm crazy having another baby. I should have had an abortion." But she carried the child to term and when it was born she christened it Sarah.

Anne and Diane left the CBC and started up their own casting agency. Kevin became one of their biggest clients. And Sarah became the star of *Road to Avonlea*. After Diane died, Anne called me to say she was swamped and asked me if I could come in and help her for a week or two. I stayed for about six months, working on several shows (without pay). It was interesting work and put me in occasional contact with Kevin. I discovered that his story editor was a former student of mine, Debbie Nathan. I went to see her with outlines for two episodes for the series. She told me that she thought they had potential. A few days later, Kevin called me to say that he was not going to accept my ideas. "It's not that they aren't any good, but I don't want you working for me. I have a long fuse but when I blow up it isn't pretty. You were my mentor and I don't want you to see that." And he hung up.

Some weeks later, Anne and I went together to the annual television conference in Banff. One morning at breakfast Kevin came to my table and after a bit of amiable chatter asked me if I was going to continue working on casting with Anne. I said I thought not. Two weeks later, he sent Anne notice that he was going to engage another casting director. Anne had already asked me to come into partnership with her. She was thinking of working less. She hoped I would invest in her company. I discussed this with Arthur Gelgoot, my accountant, who told me that the company wasn't worth anything. Its only value consisted of Anne's contacts.

I weighed the idea and decided against it. It offered a chance to be in the film business, but the hours were long and often involved a good deal of overtime. And the financial rewards were meagre. Once in awhile there was the excitement of talking to a real star. At one point Kevin wanted to hire Lauren

Bacall to play a sort of Lady Bracknell–style dowager. She hesitated and, about a week before the shoot began, turned down the offer. Disney had to approve any guest stars and they decided the next most desirable woman was Diana Rigg. I got to call her in London.

"You're offering how much?" It was half the fee we had stipulated for Bacall. "Yes, darling, I could do that."

"Shall I send you a script, Miss Rigg?"

"Oh, no. If I'm going to be away for a week I'll have to take Archie fishing in Scotland this weekend. Meet me at the airport with the script on Tuesday. I'll read it on the way to my hotel and tell you which lines I'm not prepared to say."

But encounters with glamorous people were rare. More often I would get a call from some producer to say, "I need a pair of Chinese twins who can fit a size-three dress for tomorrow afternoon." By this time I had already established myself as a writer, and I knew if I worked in casting I would have to put that aside. I bade Anne farewell and we remained friends, which might not have been the case if we had become partners. I had learned that Anne was a demanding perfectionist. She had tolerated my freewheeling ways but I could see that it irked her, and sooner or later she would have given voice to her objections and there would have to be a showdown.

At this time, I used to go to London every year, usually in the spring. I would stay with my friend Powell at the vicarage where he lived with his partner, Peter, who was an Anglican clergyman. His close friend Rodney Archer was a frequent visitor. Rodney and Powell had written several plays, one of which was about Jack the Ripper. It was performed by candlelight in an abandoned synagogue and won an award. We decided we would collaborate on writing a television series about an extended family that had branches in England, Canada, and the United States. The characters included Russian émigrés, Native Americans, and their horses. We wrote two or three episodes over a period of year, mailing scripts back and forth and editing each other's work.

Ronald Bryden set up a meeting for me with Peggy Ramsay, then one of the most influential agents in London. She agreed to see me in her office. She sat at a desk crowded with papers and swivelled around in her chair, jangling an armful of bracelets and hiking up her tweed skirt to give me a full view of her knickers. She was very jolly and gossipy, but when I outlined our idea she said it was much too tame for her. She did, however, allow me to stand her lunch at a fashionable restaurant where she was greeted by a number of chums, including Simon Callow.

I took the outline and the completed scripts to a producer I knew at the CBC but was told that they were already shooting a period drama about an upscale Montreal family called *Chasing Rainbows*. It would air the next season and would start the career of Canadian actor Paul Gross. In England, Powell and Rodney managed to get the scripts to producer Patrick Dromgoole, who at the time had influence with the BBC.

In spite of the fact that I had been offered a chance to join a workshop on writing comedy for television at the CBC, I flew to London instead to take a meeting with Patrick. It was extremely brief. After the exchange of a few courtesies, he turned to us and said, "I've read your scripts. I'm going to pass. Frankly, what you're attempting has been done before and done better. Good day." So my hopes of making a fortune writing for television crashed to the ground. At least for the time being.

My friend Richard Monette once said to me, "I don't know why you think you want to work in the film business. Everyone in it is a crook." My experience would prove he was not entirely wrong.

SCHOOL FOR GOSSIPS

It didn't take me long after I left the university to realize I was not going to be able to make a living as a theatre director.

I had always thought of myself as a writer and I determined to pursue this as my next career (either my third or fourth, depending on whether you count my brief time as a boy diplomat). I decided that I should write something that got printed and paid for if I wanted to be taken seriously. The obvious outlet for my writing efforts was journalism. During my trip around the world in the early '80s I had written a couple of travel pieces based on my time in Hong Kong and, later, Singapore. I sent these to Robert Fulford, who was then the editor of *Saturday Night*, and he responded, saying he thought they had some merit although they were not suitable for his magazine. I would soon learn this was a standard response from an editor who was not really interested in my work.

At about this time I had a meeting with Robertson Davies, who encouraged me in my journalistic ambitions. He had of course been a journalist himself, first as a columnist for *Saturday Night* and then as the editor of the *Peterborough Examiner*, where he introduced the character of Samuel Marchbanks. Davies told me that I could expect to become a competent journalist in six months and a skilled one by the end of eighteen months but that I might find, as he had, that the work became repetitive by the end of six or seven years. But first I had to get started.

I approached Barbara Sutton, a long-time friend of my wife Judith, whose family had a cottage just down the shore from our cottage at Marshall Bay. We had been acquainted briefly at Trinity College when I edited the weekly rag *Salterrae*, which contained a column by one of the young ladies of our sister college, St. Hilda's, under the heading of "Saints' Sagacity." Barbara wrote that weekly section, which my friend Troop and I often edited in a rather scabrous fashion. Our undergraduate ribaldry extended to renaming the column on one occasion to "Saints' Sagassity" and on another to "Snatches Snitched from Snilda's" ("snatch" being, at the time, slang for female genitalia). Barbara must surely have been at the very least annoyed by our smartass mauling of her prose. However, when I approached her to see if she would be willing to give me an introduction to the editors of the magazine for which she was working as copy editor, she graciously agreed, whether out of friendship for my wife or pure Christian charity, I was never certain.

The publication was *City & Country Home*, an upscale magazine about home decoration published by Maclean Hunter. I met with the features editor, Charles Oberdorff, and we immediately hit it off. Charles was a cultivated American with a knowledgeable interest in theatre and the arts. He declined to accept the travel pieces I showed him but gave me a commission to write an incidental piece comparing the Shaw and Stratford festivals. This was right down my alley, as Charles must have known. I produced a short essay in which I compared the two festivals to royal courts; Christopher Newton's regime in Niagara I likened to the Versailles of Louis XIV, while Hirsch's fief at Stratford I compared to the papacy of the Borgias. Charles was delighted with this bit of overblown extravagance and, as neither of the directors objected, I have to assume that they found it amusing.

I would continue to write occasional pieces for this magazine for a number of years — travel pieces about New York and Sweden, pieces about dance and theatre, pieces about visual art and books and antiques, and brief profiles of actors and decorators and visual artists. The fees for this work were modest and Charles let me know that if I wanted to make more money I should try covering various house visits, which provided the main articles in the magazine. This involved working with the editor Barbara Jean. We had lunch together and we got along well. The fact that we both enjoyed a glass or two of wine proved a bond.

Initially I was concerned about my lack of expertise in the field, but I discovered that I could in fact recognize a Sheraton chair or diamond-front Quebecois armoire. During the next few years, I wrote pieces about a variety of habitats, from the luxurious London quarters of the Canadian hostess Belle Shenkman to the elegant Montreal apartment of antique dealer Michel Taschereau, or the New York pad of Canadian Consul General Robert Johnstone and his art-collecting wife Popsy; from the neo-Georgian Rosedale residence of Bill and Cathy Graham to the rural stone farmhouse of my longtime friend Elsie Densem; from the apartment in Lower Town Quebec city of my friend Bill Glassco to Scotts Symons' country showplace east of Toronto. Some of these were assignments I was given, and others were friends whom

I persuaded to let me invade their privacy; occasionally they were less than pleased with what I wrote, but no one threatened to sue me.

One of my most amusing assignments was a mansion that had been built by a Quebecois millionaire businessman for his daughter, who had married a policeman from Hull. The house was loaded with elaborate nineteenth-century bric-a-brac in what I can only described as the most florid taste. While the photographer was shooting the salon and dining room, my hostess asked me if I wanted to see the bedroom. I knew we would not be shooting it but I couldn't resist. She led me to a large room featuring a king-sized tassel-draped canopy bed on a dais, with a magnificent view overlooking the Ottawa River. On the facing wall was a portrait on black velvet of a curvaceous nude. When she saw me eyeing it, my hostess exclaimed, "Jacques' mistress. Not bad, *hein*?"

Having established myself as a regular contributor to *City & Country Home*, I looked to broaden my base. I was on friendly terms with Michael de Pencier, the owner of *Toronto Life*. When I approached him he told me he never interfered with the hiring policies of his staff but he would ask his editor Marq de Villiers to meet with me. Marq was a South African with an amused and tolerant view of his fellow creatures. Our initial interview went well. I queried him about the spelling of his first name, which he admitted was an early affectation. Once on a cruise ship in the Mediterranean when he had booked into tourist class, a steward had appeared at the door of his stateroom to say, "*M. le Marquis, s'il vous plait, suivez-moi*," and promptly installed him a first class cabin. He decided there and then to stick with the q.

About a week after my initial meeting with Marq he called me to say they were planning an issue built around stories about various Toronto establishments: medical, legal, financial, academic, and social. He had been intending to write on this last group himself but suggested that I might like to take a crack at it.

I produced a piece that looked at Toronto's upper crust, starting with the Simcoes and the Jarvises and moving on to the Masseys and the Flavelles. It was filled with somewhat racy anecdotes: how Aemilius Jarvis was allowed to take his horse and his valet with him when he went to prison for fraud, how Prince Nachashadze was arrested by police as he was about to lead his daughter down the aisle, how Scott Symons failed to appear at a dance given by his father-in-law to show that Scott and his daughter were still together, but in his place sent four transvestites who performed an outrageous dance for the shocked amusement of the assembled company.

I pointed out that most of the FOOFs (Fine Old Ontario Families) had started out as farmers and consequently it counted for more in social circles if your ancestors worked the land than if you had made a fortune on Bay Street. The piece was widely read and even extensively quoted. I found it rather ironic that a middle-class boy from suburban North Toronto was suddenly seen as something of an expert on Toronto society.

This essay also established me as a regular contributor to *Toronto Life*. I came to understand that the principles of salesmanship that I had learned selling paper to printers worked equally well when I was trying to peddle ideas for magazine articles. First, you must have a valid product; second, you must figure out who is likely to buy it; third, you must establish a relationship with the prospective buyer. With both Charles and Marq I was able to connect; we enjoyed each other's company and frequently lunched together and gossiped about the trade, politics, and the world of the arts.

I would write a number of feature articles for *Toronto Life:* A piece on the specialized bookstores that were then extant in the city before the advent of Chapters and Indigo drove them out of business. A piece on Greg Gatenby and the Authors Festival he created at Harbourfront. A piece on cultural building projects, such as Roy Thomson Hall and the projected opera house. A profile of my friend Morden Yolles, who, as a structural engineer, collaborated with some of the best architects in the city including Ron Thom and Moshe Safdie.

It seemed logical to me that I should write about theatre but I was told that this was the exclusive territory of Martin Knelman, who had made it clear I was not to trespass on his turf. I would encounter similar claims of exclusivity in the future.

I formed a good working relationship with Jocelyn Laurence, the daughter of novelist Margaret Laurence, who was a senior editor at *Toronto Life*. She suggested various topics to me, but not all of my efforts made it into print. At one point Jocelyn asked me to write a piece about the programs for gifted children that were then being set up in the city's high schools. I concluded that this was an attempt on the part of the board of education to enrich their curriculum and provide competition to the private schools.

Jocelyn was not pleased with my approach. She had wanted me to attack the "gifted programs" as elitist. On another occasion I was asked to write a piece about Michael Levine and his influence as a promoter of various artists, including Veronica Tennant and Adrienne Clarkson. I approached Michael, whom I already knew, and he agreed to let me interview him about his ongoing relationship with Patrick Watson, the television producer and CBC executive. However, my editor complained that there was too much about Watson in the finished piece, and it also ended up in the round file.

One of my more successful efforts was a profile of Isadore Sharpe, the founder of the Four Seasons chain of hotels. Mr. Sharpe granted me an interview. We chatted amiably for half an hour, at which point I said, "Thank you, I think I have what I need."

"But you haven't taken any notes," exclaimed Mr. Sharpe. Shortly after the piece appeared, I received a note from him to say that this was the most accurate piece that had ever been written about him.

I had a good memory, but also I had learned that if you don't take notes or use a tape recorder, an interviewee will often speak much more freely and confidentially. Although I had figured this out on my own, I later learned that Truman Capote had pioneered this technique, which he used to great effect when he interviewed Marlon Brando for the *New Yorker* and succeeded in getting the actor to spill a lot of secrets about his sex life.

Jocelyn moved to the editorship of *Canadian Art*, another publication inaugurated by Michael de Pencier in conjunction with Anna Porter. Her colleagues included Susan Walker and Sarah Milroy. They commissioned me to do several pieces, including a history of the growth of the Hart House art collection (the first significant assembly of works by the Group of Seven) and also a study of three important Canadian animators: Norman McLaren, George Dunning, and my old friend Richard Williams. I was able to visit Montreal and obtain the last interview McLaren gave before his death. I also did profiles of Canadian stage designers Michael Levine and Martha Mann. I suggested a piece on a farm boy from near Arnprior who was having a great success selling his paintings of roosters, but although my trio of editors were amused by the idea, they failed to publish it.

In order to expand my scope, I approached various other magazines including *Moneywise* and *Chatelaine*, both published by Maclean Hunter, and the country lifestyle magazine *Harrowsmith*. Although I managed to sell a couple of articles, my knowledge of the areas that they covered was insufficiently specific. I recall that I wrote articles for *Moneywise* about the careers of actor Richard Monette and real estate super-saleslady Sis Weld that were rejected because there was not enough data about their earnings. I was able to rejig both articles and sell them elsewhere. I did not feel in the least guilty about this. I had learned that I would often suggest story ideas to editors that they would reject, only to offer them to other writers to execute. But in spite of this I enjoyed the company of the people I met in the fraternity of journalists who loved to get together and trade stories over a glass or two of vino.

One of my father's partners was a man called Wilf Parmelee who ran our Ottawa office and warehouse. He had a pretty and animated daughter, Helen, whom I had escorted years before to the External Affairs winter ball. She married Peter Worthington and pursued a career as a journalist in her own right. She called me one day to say she thought she had an opening for me and asked me to meet her at the offices of the *Toronto Star*. She informed me they were going to launch an upscale weekly supplement called *Elegance*, and introduced me to the managing editor. Maureen was a woman in her mid-forties with bright red hair and an elaborate *maquillage*. She wore a low-necked dress, the edge of which betrayed traces of body makeup. Her conversational style was colourful and peppered with some rather ripe phrases. She took me to lunch along with her factotum, a rather timid middle-aged Brit. With Maureen in the lead we swept into an expensive restaurant where we were greeted effusively by the maître d'. Maureen disdained to look over the menu and commanded, "James, order me lunch." James obliged while Maureen told me she had been impressed by my article on Toronto society and felt certain I was the perfect person to help her launch her new project.

She commissioned me to write an initial article on the horsey set in Toronto. Although I knew nothing about this milieu I was able to consult a number of sources as varied as Michael Sifton, Toronto's leading polo player, whom I had known in grade school; Norman Elder, who with his brother had ridden for Canada in international competitions; and my friend John Uren, who was a devotee of the racetrack. I put together a piece which was full of colourful detail and was the lead article in the first edition of *Elegance*. An acquaintance who hunted regularly pronounced it "really quite sound for someone who had no firsthand knowledge of the subject." I followed this piece with one on the sailing community and others about gardening, charity balls, and gentleman farmers in Caledon. There were also profiles of prominent women such as Pauline McGibbon and Doris Anderson.

It was suggested I do a piece on Sondra Gotlieb, the wife of the Canadian ambassador to the United States, who had just made news by publicly slapping her social secretary at an embassy reception. Somewhat to my surprise, Mrs. Gotlieb agreed to an interview and I was dispatched to Washington where I was to meet up with a photographer, who failed to put in an appearance. My interviewee showed up an hour late and was furious to learn that there was no photographer, as she had just spent the last two hours with her hairdresser. Fortunately I had the wit to phone United Press, who agreed to send one of their staff forthwith. The lady calmed down and was actually quite charming. I was interested to learn that she had written a comic novel, *True Confections*, about growing up as a Jewish girl in Winnipeg. In fact it was just being shot as a movie by my friend Gail Singer, and so we had something to talk about till the photographer arrived. It turned out she was actually pleased with the piece, and so was Maureen.

My brother-in-law, David Lewis Stein, who was a columnist at the *Star*, informed me at about this time that they were looking for a new drama critic. I was duly interviewed and told I certainly had the background but did not have enough experience as a newspaper journalist. I was therefore passed over in favour of someone who was already on the staff. I had mixed feelings about this. I had not completely given up my theatrical ambitions and, had I become a critic, it would undoubtedly have given me increased clout in the world of drama. On the other hand, I was deeply ambivalent about critics, whom I felt exercised a great deal of influence without having the knowledge of actual practice in the field and were often capricious in their judgment.

At about the same time, a free weekly newspaper, *NOW*, began appearing on the newsstands. The *Toronto Star* management felt they must compete and started to put out a weekly supplement dealing with popular entertainment. The regular staffers at the paper did not initially want to write additional columns and I was therefore commissioned to write promotional pieces and a few critiques about fringe attractions in theatre and dance. I wrote as many as three or four columns for some issues and soon piled up significant evidence of my ability to write for a daily newspaper. However, the regular columnists saw my work as a hostile invasion of their territory, and this outlet for my writing talents dried up as suddenly as it had begun.

Shortly after this, Susan Walker, one of my former editors at *Canadian Art*, was appointed temporary editor of the *Star*'s weekend entertainment supplement. At the time she was the wife of Colin Vaughan and consequently was in a strong position at the paper, where he was a regular columnist. I began writing book reviews for her, and before long she asked me to do a number of profiles of prominent people in the entertainment world. I wrote pieces about several Stratford personalities: the veteran designer Tanya Moiseiwitsch; director John Hirsch; and Richard Monette, who was just coming into his own as a director at Stratford. While researching my piece on Hirsch I spent an afternoon him at his Toronto house shortly before he died. He told me that somebody should be writing the cultural history of the performing arts in Canada and suggested that I might be a good candidate to do this.

The idea would stay with me. Before long Susan was replaced by a new literary editor at the *Star* and although I continued to do the odd book review, I was no longer in demand as a columnist.

I was asked by my long-time friend Margaret "Mugs" Macaulay to write some pieces for the *University of Toronto Magazine*. These included reminiscences of social life at the university in the '50s; a retrospective of Hart House Theatre in the glory days of director Robert Gill; and profiles of some distinguished members of the faculty, including Pia Kleber, who was leading the new University College Drama Program; Brian Stock, a medievalist at the Pontifical Institute; and my friend Andrew Watson, an economic historian with an impressive record of work as an advisor to various foundations and international agencies in Africa and the Middle East.

Soon after, I was approached by John Fraser, who took over at *Saturday Night* as editor under the new owner, Conrad Black. John asked me to write a social column and this seemed like a good fit. He edited the first piece I produced rather severely and asked me if I could live with his version. I said okay, somewhat reluctantly. The second column was to be about private men's clubs in Toronto. I handed it in and was asked by one of the editors, Barbara Moon, if I was interested in seeing the revised copy. I said yes and was horrified by the changes she had made. Then John suggested I write a piece about North Hatley, a popular resort in the eastern townships of Quebec. John performed a rigorous rewrite, and I phoned him and told him that if he wanted to write the column himself, he had better do so, but he couldn't continue to use my name. John apologized and eventually asked me to do a piece about Robin Phillips, who was at that time artistic director of the Citadel Theatre in

Edmonton. I flew to the western city in the depths of winter at Robin's invitation, only to have him tell me he was no longer giving interviews. I wrote a piece based on a radio interview I had done with him a year or two earlier. After I submitted it, the fact checker phoned to tell me Robin reported he couldn't possibly have said what I reported. I told her I had his remarks on tape. But I'd had enough of trying to deal with John's hierarchy at *Saturday Night*.

I had enjoyed a good run as a cultural journalist over a period of a decade. I had found a voice and developed a prose style, but the assignments had become somewhat repetitive and I couldn't help remembering the words spoken to me by Robertson Davies at the outset of my journalistic career. It all came to an end fairly quickly in the early 1980s. With the recession, many of the magazines I had worked for either disappeared or became much slimmer. *City & Country Home* went out of business; Marq de Villiers moved on and was replaced at *Toronto Life* by John McFarlane, who, although he received me cordially enough, did not seem interested in my proposals for articles; the *Toronto Star* decided that *Elegance* was not consistent with their image as a populist newspaper and discontinued it. Mugs Macaulay was replaced by a new editor with a less nostalgic vision of the publication. I also realized that my anecdotal style was giving way to a new fashion: less allusive and literary, shorter, sharper, tougher.

In the course of my career I was able to rack up and deduct expenses against my earnings which allowed me to live rather more lavishly than the actual pay permitted. I travelled frequently, although I rapidly discovered that the competition in travel writing was extensive and the pay consequently low. I did have a couple of very pleasant outings, especially a trip to Sweden, an account of which I will reprint below. I went frequently to New York and London, where I often had lunch with my old friend Robert Troop, then the editor of a successful trade paper about real estate. Over lunch at the Café Royal in Regent Street, we recalled our early ambitions to be writers of serious literature. "I've become the foremost property journalist in Britain, which certainly isn't what I originally had in mind," lamented Robert. "And I've become one of the most successful gossip columnists in Canada," I responded. "Oh well, I suppose it's better than nothing.' And we drowned our thwarted ambitions in a bottle of Nuits-Saint-Georges.

NASTY SURPRISE

In the second summer of my Youtheatre season, one of the participants was a tall, chunky, towheaded kid with huge blue eyes called David Wilkinson, who auditioned with his friend Sheila Russell. They did a silly skit of their own devising and although it didn't display any great acting ability, I was always a sucker for someone who could make me laugh, so we accepted them into the company. That summer we did productions of both *Romeo and Juliet* and *Much Ado About Nothing* in the University College quad. Sheila, who had been in the company the year before, played the Nurse and Beatrice. David played Dogberry with a naive enthusiasm that brought welcome comic relief to the production. He would continue to be in my Youtheatre programs for the next few years.

David was a student at my old high school, Lawrence Park Collegiate. He had an active social life with a good many friends to whom he gave nicknames: "Fluffy Corvette," "Miss Fancyface," "Hum Dinger," and for himself, "Nasty Surprise." Academically, neither he nor the school were having a good experience. I suggested he apply to a new alternative school, SEED, whose principal was my friend Gordon Jocelyn. I don't know whether my influence gained him admission but the next thing I knew, he had talked Gordon into letting him and Sheila take my theatre class at the university for credit. This, I would learn, was typical of David's ability to wangle deals. One of the class assignments was for a group of students to present a short original script of about five minutes. David, Sheila, and one other kid offered up a short piece about three rather repulsive but funny public school kids at recess called *Smarties*, an allusion to a popular brand of candies. David was the author of the skit and I realized that although he could not spell and had only the vaguest ideas about grammar, he had potential as a writer.

David began to come to my house after classes (when he actually did attend classes.) He would sit in the kitchen while I prepared dinner and often stay to eat it with us. He was about the same age as my own kids and they took an immediate liking to him, especially my sons Guy and Ben, both of whom were natural clowns. I was a bit concerned that David's parents might wonder about his frequent absence from their dinner table, but when I got in touch with his mother, Shelagh, she told me that David seemed much happier than he had been at Lawrence and thanked me for my concern. She was a rather formidable character, an early feminist who had started a women's studies program at York University. She and her husband had decided they weren't going to have any children and adopted a baby girl. In a classic case, she discovered three months after the adoption that she was pregnant, and David was her first natural child. Two years later she had a daughter, Leslie. David got on well with his siblings but they had little in common and I think he was happy to adopt our family as almost his own.

After I left the university and embarked on a career as a journalist, I introduced David to Anita, one of my editors at the magazine *City & Country Home*. She took an immediate shine to him and he sold her on the idea that he should do a travel piece for the magazine on Italy. He knew nothing of its culture or language but had a friend in Sardinia. By this time, he had left home and was living with some other young people in a house on Carlton Street. One of the other boarders was Bernard Leroux, who had just graduated in photography from the Ontario College of Art. David introduced him to Anita as his working colleague and obtained a letter from her commissioning a series of articles. He then persuaded Alitalia to fly him and Bernard to Rome, business class.

In the years to come, David would become an expert at finagling passage from airlines, and he crossed the Atlantic many times, usually with a large hockey bag full of his clothes and other gear, which he insisted he had to have in the cabin with him. He also talked his way into accommodation at some of the world's most prestigious hotels: the Hassler in Rome; the Pierre in New York; the Villa d'Este on Lake Como; and the Crillon in Paris, where David took a shine to one of the waiters and asked if he would come to his room and have sex with him if he bought a bottle of champagne. The tactic was apparently successful. He seemed to know instinctively that the more outrageous his demands, the more likely they were to be granted.

David's initial contact in Italy was a beautiful woman who was married to a wealthy Dane who owned a villa in Sardinia. She invited David to stay with her. Sardinia was just being opened up as a holiday resort by the Aga Khan. David somehow managed to get an interview with this potentate, who was only too happy to promote his project to high-end travellers. Bernard was able to shoot some very glamorous people, and Anita was delighted with David's sharp, gossipy prose.

During his stay in Sardinia, David met a number of rich Italians, and his next target was Rome, where was able to make some valuable contacts, partly with the help of my friend Gilbert Reid, who was the cultural attaché at the Canadian Embassy. David rented a small flat near the Coliseum from the Italian husband of another friend of mine, Marta Braun, and Judy and I went to Rome and stayed with him for a week. We financed his visits to the opera at the Baths of Caracalla and several high-end restaurants, all of which he wrote up for Anita.

David returned to Canada and took up with another Youtheatre student, Laurie Brown, a very pretty girl with a fine singing voice. David was attracted to pretty women and a number of them reciprocated his interest. He was amusing, provocative, and, although not conventionally handsome, sexy. I was no longer attached to the university but I agreed, with the encouragement of the Ontario government, to continue doing Youtheatre programs. I directed two Shakespeare plays, *Twelfth Night* and *Timon of Athens* at the Glen Morris Studio. David played Sir Andrew Aguecheek in what was to be his most successful performance. He also undertook the management and publicity for the season and succeeded in getting the notoriously censorious critic Gina Mallet to come and see our shows. To our surprise, she gave us a very positive review and we did good business.

The officials of the Ontario Department of Culture and Tourism, or whatever it was called at the time, were pleased and suggested that the next summer I set up a professional and paid young company using actors just graduated from theatre schools. By this time my career as a journalist was just starting to take off and I didn't want to abandon it. My friend Juliana Saxton had just been let go by the faculty of education, where she had been teaching theatre arts. I suggested that she might like to be artistic director of this new enterprise. I offered to direct one of three shows and introduced her to David as a potential general manager.

Juliana and David hit it off, and they would work together on a number of projects in the next few years, including a one-woman show performed by Norma Edwards called *The Women of Margaret Laurence*, which toured across Canada and even visited Scandinavia. David seemed to be setting himself up for a career as a theatre administrator but, typically, he was beginning to be bored by his success in the field. He returned to Europe, where his friends from Sardinia had just rented a chalet in Gstaad, and sent home pieces about the smart set who skied in the Swiss Alps.

David's relationship with Laurie didn't last, but they remained friends. Laurie would later say that David's great talent was for friendship; if you were a friend of David's, you became and remained friends with all his other friends. Laurie, Sheila Russell, and Bernard Leroux are still my friends. David's relationship with Sheila was in some ways his closest. As well as coming to my classes, they enrolled in Barry Flatman's classes at Homemade Theatre where they honed their skills in broad comedy or, as they described it, "making faces." They played elaborate tricks on each other, making dates to meet but not turning up, leaving a note stuck to a lamppost or an article in the window of a store. On one occasion, Sheila drove David out into the country on a winter night. When he got out of the car to take a pee, she drove off, leaving him to hitchhike home.

This behaviour was closely related to David's subversive attitude towards authority in all its guises. He loved to point to the pee-stains on the trousers of a pompous professor or to expose the inconsistency in the arguments of his mother's feminist cohorts. He once attended one of her meetings in drag and promoted equal rights for transsexuals at a time when most people didn't even know that trannies existed. He could never resist taking the piss out of the pretentious, even when, or perhaps especially when, they were long-time friends.

David was bisexual. He loved and pursued beautiful women, who were attracted by his offbeat charm and his avant-garde appearance (he dressed in the latest fashion and, when he discovered he was losing his hair, shaved his skull, long before this became a common practice.) He had an extended affair with a considerably older Irishwoman, one of his mother's acolytes. But he was unwilling to make a permanent commitment to anybody. When one of his liaisons resulted in a pregnancy, he adamantly insisted on an abortion. His frequent encounters with men were casual and never led to an extended relationship, although a few of his male partners became long-term friends.

During one of his not infrequent spats with his strong-minded mother, David moved in with us on Sherbourne Street. He would often sit in the kitchen while I was making the dinner, and we would listen to recordings of female black singers. I had several records with titles like *The Ladies of Jazz*. We would test each other's knowledge by trying to identify Ella Fitzgerald, Bessie Smith, Billie Holiday, Dinah Washington, Sarah Vaughan, Alberta Hunter, and Nina Simone. David soon began to make dishes for supper, sometimes quite elaborate. He had taken a cooking course on one of his excursions to France. He also invented alternative lyrics for some of the standards we listened to. He said he and Laurie were going to put out an album of "Herb Hits": "Thyme on My Hands," "I'll Never Forget Sweet Marjoram," "You're My Dill."

It was during one of these sessions of cooking to music that we had a brainwave. We would write a musical. It was called *Baby Grand*. The title character was an aging lounge singer who takes up with a young songwriter who visits her club. They go off together for a gig in Florida. Meanwhile, his former girlfriend, Steve, is asked by the club owner to fill in for Baby and she becomes a huge hit. It was a simple little piece with a somewhat bittersweet ending: Baby comes back to the club and the young singer, Steve, and the songwriter reconnect.

That summer David came up to Judy's cottage at Marshall Bay and we began to write some scenes. In the piece we included standards*: Here I Go Again, I Got It Bad,* and *Just One of Those Things*, among others, but we needed some original songs. David hooked us up with his friend John Roby, an accomplished pianist with a track record of writing songs for musicals, and he wrote a number of tunes for which I supplied the lyrics. The best of these, *Sea Story*, had a life even after *Baby Grand* was forgotten.

I went with you on a rolling ride,
Riding with the tide
To the centre of the sea:
You were by my side,
Lying with your eyes;
You set us drifting free.
And somewhere above you
A sea breeze whispered love you, love you . . .

When I awoke you were far away,
Wading in the waves
At the edge of the sea.
I watched you walk away,

Wondered what to say
And what came over me.

David had a connection with Bob White, the artistic director of Factory Lab Theatre, who agreed to let us do a trial production in his smaller space. I was able to talk David Rotenburg, a former student of mine, into coming up from New York and directing. He had some experience with musicals and insisted on vetting the cast and also supervising revisions of the book. David and I had written it together. Both Davids were quite critical of my work, but I assumed responsibility for stitching the various scenes together and in the end the book was quite tight and amusing without being just a series of gags.

We were lucky to assemble a good cast. Jennifer Phipps agreed to play Baby; she did not have a great singing voice, but as Baby was on her way out, this was not a drawback. Her delivery was stylish and original and she provided the play with its emotional heart. Laurie Brown played the young singer Steve. She looked great and had a strong singing voice. Her acting style was cool and provided an effective contrast to Jennifer's erratic exuberance. Richard Greenblatt was the young composer. A sexy young guy and an expert pianist, he played the role with charm and a light touch. Julie, the club manager was an older actor with an easy-going manner. The show played two weeks at Factory and attracted young audiences who enjoyed the music and laughed at the contemporary if somewhat superficial dialogue.

David Rotenburg's father, a doctor, came to see the show and talked with David about funding a production. David dissuaded him, saying he would only lose money. This was disappointing, but my subsequent experiences producing theatre in Toronto confirmed the wisdom of David's judgment. We thought that one of the alternate theatres might pick up our show. I sent the script to Urjo Kareda, who wrote back saying, "I thought the young couple were gay lovers, but when I realized Steve was a girl, I lost interest." We did do a promising workshop with Susan Wright taking on the role of Baby and Ted Dykstra as the young songwriter. They would have given the play a stronger, more positive slant. Susan was an accomplished singer and at that point Ted was not only a fine pianist but a very cute kid. Tragically, Susan perished in a fire not long after. We felt fate had slammed the lid on *Baby Grand*.

Then the next summer Jeff Braunstein, one of the founding partners of Homemade Theatre, where David had been a student, approached us. He had been asked by the Sheraton Hotel to put together a couple of shows for a summer dinner theatre that they wanted to initiate in a dining room on their second floor. Jeff thought *Baby Grand* would fill the bill. Neither John Roby nor Richard Greenblatt were available, but Jennifer and Laurie agreed to do their original roles. Richard was replaced by another actor who was a capable pianist, though he lacked Richard's boyish charm. There was little time for rehearsals but the show opened. It was reviewed by Ray Conlogue, the *Globe and Mail*'s theatre critic and a former student of mine. It was not a pan but was condescending and suggested the play needed a thorough rewrite, but this is not what sunk it. Some of the audience members complained to the hotel that this was not their idea of a fun evening in the theatre. The character of Baby was depressing, even though she has a moment of self-realization at the end, where she returns to Julie, her long-time manager, and sings to him:

> I always thought that I was smart
> My head was clear, my dear,
> And ruled my heart
> You watched me chasing
> Some new lover
> I was unaware
> Time would blow my cover,
> Leave me hanging in the air.
> The mirror cracked;
> I came to see
> My little act, in fact
> Fooled nobody but me.
> The game is done.
> I'm wiser now,
> I see it's true.
> The one who understood the game
> Was you.

The show ran for a week and closed.

A year or so later I went to a party where I met Tammy Grimes, who was playing Madame Arcati in a production of Noël Coward's *Blithe Spirit* at the Royal Alex. She took a shine to me and invited me up to her hotel room at the Windsor Arms, where we had a brief intimate encounter. She dragged on a cigarette and said, "So, Mr. Playwright, do you have a script for me?" Suddenly I thought of *Baby Grand*. I took it around to her hotel the next day. Two days later, she called me. She liked the script and could see herself doing it. I realized she was serious. I approached several producers whom I knew slightly, but none of them were sufficiently interested to step up to the plate. Tammy returned to New York. We kept in touch for a bit. I realized that she would have done the show if I had been able to get up a production. This would eventually lead me to become a producer of my own work, with less than stunning results.

David and I flew to Spain on a joint assignment for *City & Country Home* and *Elegance*. We landed in Malaga, picked up a car, and drove to Torremolinos. David lobbied me to give him five hundred dollars so that he could go off on his own if he wanted and also treat me to dinner once in a while. Knowing that otherwise he would be constantly hitting me up for cash, I agreed. On our first night we sat on a terrace watching a dancer in a grey skirt and blue blazer gyrate provocatively to flamenco music. David recognized the dancer was a transvestite. Welcome to the new Spain. They went off together and left me to have a solitary brandy.

Two days later we drove up through the Sierra Nevada towards Granada. David wanted to drive. Several of us had tried to teach him and he had failed the exam in Canada three times. But the traffic on the road in Spain was light, and I thought it would be good practice for him. The road soon became steep and winding. Several times David rounded turns at breakneck speed, often swerving to the wrong side of the road. After about fifty kilometres I could stand it no longer. I took over and we reached Granada safely. We spent the next day at the Alhambra, marvelling at its splendour: the intricate carving and patterns of blue and green tiles, the majestic courts with their splashing fountains, and the elegant gardens where tall cypresses and blossoming oleanders looked down on beds of roses and the air was heavy with the scent of jasmine. We went to a service in the cathedral dedicated to Isabel la Católica, the queen who expelled the Moors from Spain and forced the conversion of the Spanish Jews. The people of Granada were campaigning the Pope to canonize her in time for the five hundredth anniversary of Columbus's discovery of the New World, an expedition financed by the queen pawning her jewels, or so we had been taught in grade five.

From Granada we drove north to Barcelona where we were greeted by David Fulton and Gloria Montero, whose daughter Allegra was a long-time friend. They put us up in their colourful apartment on a little street steps from La Rambla. David was an Australian who had been a CBC producer before he and Gloria retired to Spain. Gloria was a writer of fiction and stage plays. They were fluent in both Spanish and Catalan. They knew Barcelona well and took us to some of their favourite haunts: the restaurant Taxidermista in a courtyard in the old city, and the Liceu opera house where we heard Montserrat Caballé, whom David dubbed "Monsterfat Caballera." On Fulton's recommendation we visited Sagrada Família, the Gaudí cathedral still under construction; the Picasso, Miró, and Dali museums; and the old church of Santa Maria del Mar.

David also explored the baths, where a number of Moroccan and Algerian boys were available for hire. He insisted we go to a gay dance hall called Martin's, where a lot of handsome young men, many of them stripped to the waist, and a few women (or were they drag queens?) twisted and twirled on the dance floor. David disappeared into the back room. By two o'clock I had run out of interest and went home. An hour and a half later David appeared, looking haggard. His wallet had been stolen while he had been involved in feeling up some young man. I looked at him rather sourly and said, "Why am I not surprised?" He countered by insisting he needed another five hundred dollars for the rest of our expedition.

The next day we set out for Sitges, a beach resort just south of Barcelona. It was the most openly gay town I had ever experienced. Guys picked each other up in bars, on the beach, in the street. We booked into the Romance Hotel, a slightly ramshackle converted mansion full of ancient gilt and marble furniture, and walls decorated with enormous erotic paintings. We spent the day at the beach, ate in a waterside restaurant, and then set out to tour the bars. They were crowded with scantily dressed men, many sporting makeup, feathers, and sequins. We moved from one watering hole to the next until finally, at about two o'clock, I retired to bed.

At about four David showed up in our room with two companions. One was a diminutive German wearing a jockstrap and a choker blazing with stones, which he insisted were real diamonds. The other was a lanky American with long, slightly thinning blond hair. He explained that he was covering Sitges for a gay magazine published in Boston. Although he had a girlfriend in Montreal, he and his publisher were lovers and had vowed to have sex together in every state in the union. Their current count was thirty-eight. He had already written about the other major gay resorts: the Greek island of Mykonos, Pattaya in Thailand, Puerto Vallarta on the Pacific coast of Mexico, and of course Provincetown across the harbour from Boston.

The German guy produced a bottle of schnapps. I had two or three shots before I passed out. When I woke in the morning they were all gone, including David, who turned up about ten o'clock having spent the intervening hours with the American. While David slept, I went down to the beach with a book. He joined me at about four. I thought he might want another night in the bars, but he suggested we take the train back to Barcelona. We had an early flight the next morning to Madrid.

I had visited Madrid many years earlier when it was a rather sleepy town under the yoke of Franco, who rode through the town in an armoured car, surrounded by his Moroccan guard mounted on splendid stallions whose hooves were painted gold. Now the streets were full of people. At eleven in the morning, the señoras gathered at fashionable pastry shops for hot chocolate or consommé, which seemed to have replaced coffee as a morning pick-me-up. They gossiped and showed off their elegantly understated finery. In the evenings, groups of men and women walked the streets for the traditional evening *paseo*, stopping at bars to drink a glass of fino and enjoy savoury tapas. We visited the great picture collections at the Prado and the newly opened Reina Sofía museum. I spent several hours looking at the elongated saints of El Greco and the powerful, dark war paintings of Goya. And I renewed my acquaintance with Picasso's *Guernica*, which I had first seen many years before when it was hanging in the Museum of Modern Art in New York.

We spent our final night in Madrid at a redecorated movie palace that had been converted to a giant dance hall. The music was an eclectic mix: American house, Argentinian tangos, old Beatles songs, and flamenco. Chic Madrid youngsters took it all in their stride. At about one in the morning, the floor cleared as a drag queen with an enormous beehive hairdo swung into an elaborate show-off turn; at the end she tore off her dress to reveal a low-cut bustier and lacy panties whose garters barely held up laddered net stockings. As the crowd cheered, a kid near me identified the performer as the filmmaker Pedro Almodóvar.

When we got back to Toronto, David and I both went to have blood tests.

I was given a clean bill of heath, but David learned that he was HIV positive. "It's not going to make any difference to the way I live," he said. He launched into a spirited rendition of "Non, je ne regrette rien" as we sat at lunch at Arlequin, a favourite restaurant across the road from his parents' condo at "Av & Dav" (Avenue Road and Davenport). He ordered a house salad and began taking it apart and laying out the ingredients on the table. "House salad: this is the hall, this the kitchen, and this is the bathroom." The waiter looked on without amusement.

David's adopted sister was a doctor and she attempted to put him on a regime of pills and tests. David told her, "Butt out. It's my disease and I'm going to manage it myself." His parents gave him the use of their condo and he installed himself there and filled the rooms with dried flowers so that it soon resembled a sort of Bower of Bliss designed by Miss Havisham. There he entertained his close friends and a variety of hustlers he picked up in the streets. His behaviour was becoming increasingly erratic but his old friends remained supportive.

David's last European expedition involved a visit to Berlin where he succeeded in getting an interview with Canadian painter Attila Lukacs, whose sado-masochistic canvases he described in such vivid detail that the article he wrote for *Canadian Art* expurgated it. David threatened to sue, but could not afford the fee demanded by his lawyer.

A week later I received a call from Claridge's Hotel in London, where David had wangled a three-night stay. The manager called to say that David had rung up an account of over three hundred pounds. He had also had a party in his room, for which he had bought and lit some sixty candles, setting off a smoke alarm, which caused the fire department to appear in the lobby, causing consternation among the hotel's guests. The manager was anxious to get rid of David but wanted his money. Apparently David had said I would wire money to settle his bill. I sent three hundred and fifty pounds. The manager called again to say that when the money had arrived, David had promptly gone to the bar and spent the thirty-two pounds that remained after his debt had been discharged. He then called a taxi and, when it arrived, grabbed the doorman's silk topper and rode away in the cab tipping his hat and waving regally to the amused onlookers.

When David returned to Toronto he moved in with us. He had asked me to sublet his parents' condo. I gave the place a thorough cleaning and threw out all his dried flowers. He was furious about this but pleased that I had found a tenant. He had lost about thirty pounds and his cheekbones almost protruded from his skin, but with his enormous blue eyes and shaved skull he presented an exotic appearance. He insisted on wearing shorts although his legs were like matchsticks. I offered to take him to lunch at Arlequin, but when he sent the water back to the kitchen claiming it was stale, the manager asked us to leave and not come back.

David outlined his plans for the future. He insisted we should write a new musical for Laurie; it would again be about a singer, this time named Angel Cake. David insisted that, as this was his idea, his name should appear ahead of mine and indeed over the title. I tried to piece together a first act, which David presented to John Roby and his wife Patricia Vanstone, who was to direct. They tried to tell David tactfully that they didn't think the piece was viable. He informed them that not only did he not require their services, but he would be seeking a new writing partner.

David informed the press that he was setting up a series of talks by visiting gay writers. He went to New York and came back saying he had lined up Tony Kushner and Joel Grey. He hired the Firehall Theatre and a few tickets were sold. We assembled in the theatre and waited, but Kushner did not appear. David came out on stage with Laurie they and sang "Pennies from Heaven." The audience was made up of David's friends who knew his situation and did not ask for their money back.

He then called a press conference to promote the Barnes collection of master paintings that was visiting the Art Gallery of Ontario. He had somehow managed to persuade the curator that this would provide him with valuable publicity. A few members of the critical fraternity arrived at the appointed hour of eleven o'clock. For some of them it would be their first chance to see the collection. David put in an appearance some twenty minutes late. He was wearing a long blond wig and high-heeled boots. He identified himself as Erik von Bedderfeld. He persuaded his friend Bernard Leroux to film the group as he proceeded to walk the critics through the gallery, commenting in a badly feigned German accent on the pictures, many of which he disparaged in highfalutin art-speak. The curator stared at David like a terrified rabbit mesmerized by a cobra. He heaved a sigh of relief when the tour was over and the critics departed. David told me I could take him to lunch at the Four Seasons.

David had tried to persuade *City & Country Home* to run his Barnes Story.

When they rejected the idea, he simply lied to the curator. He had hoped his article, which I don't believe was ever written, would somehow create a legacy for him and also a windfall of cash. When the curator phoned the magazine editors and learned the truth, he was outraged, and the magazine wrote David off as a contributor. His writing career was over.

Not long after this, David was hospitalized. I visited him several times and was quizzed about the amount of his estate; he was planning a bequest to Casey House, which had recently been set up by June Callwood, a long-time colleague of his mother. Many of David's friends came to see him: Laurie, Sheila Russell, John Roby, Bernard Leroux, and others. I was at the cottage when Sheila Wilkinson phoned to tell me David had died. She had visited him one afternoon. He sat up in bed and sang with her Blake's "Jerusalem" and then he was gone. Sheila arranged a funeral for him at Christ Church Deer Park. The church was packed. Several of us were asked to speak. I read a Shakespeare sonnet and Blake's "The Tyger." We walked from the church to Mount Pleasant Cemetery. David's wooden coffin, made by a friend, was lowered into the earth and we all shovelled dirt into the grave.

David, more than any of my other students, had become a close friend and a sort of surrogate son. We successfully collaborated on a number of projects in spite of his somewhat prickly character and unsparing criticism of me and almost everyone he knew. But he made us all laugh. My friends, my family, we all agreed: David was one of the funniest people we had ever known.

SERENDIPITY IN SWEDEN

I was a bit surprised when the phone rang and Sue Polanyi invited me to a celebratory *conversazione* hastily improvised for her husband, John, who had just been awarded the Nobel Prize for Chemistry. I was no longer one of the university's elect, having made my exit from the faculty four year earlier, but the Polanyis were friends, so I willingly made my way to the presidential mansion, where the lights were ablaze and the flower of the city's intelligentsia were gathered to bask in the reflected limelight and congratulate themselves on this ultimate recognition of Canadian intellectual prowess. Attendees included financial patriarch Walter Gordon, department store heiress and fundraising doyenne Mary Alice Stuart, cultural caryatid Sis Bunting Weld, satirical-symbolical-chauvinist painter Charles Pachter, reforming politico-turned-social-historian William Kilbourn, and media provocateurs Patrick Watson and Adrienne Clarkson. Just being at this gathering affirmed I had a place, however minimal, in Toronto's socio-intellectual hierarchy.

After John Polanyi's graceful, self-deprecating remarks, we toasted the new laureate in acrid Niagara champagne and raised our voices in a modestly rousing rendition of "For He's a Jolly Good Fellow" before moving on to some serious networking. I found myself chatting with my old friend Tom Delworth, home on leave from his post as our ambassador in Stockholm. "I'm encouraging people to come and see John get his prize. There'll be a party of at least a dozen. Why don't you and Judy climb aboard? You'll love Sweden. It's one of the few truly civilized countries left in the world."

In fact, we didn't join the party of well-wishers who accompanied the Polanyis to Stockholm, but we picked up on Tom's invitation a few months later when I had put together a string of freelance journalistic assignments in England and France and thought it might be interesting to tack Sweden onto the end of my junket. It would be a chance for a bit of a holiday and I just might finagle free airfare if I could figure out an angle for a story. Tom suggested I check out a conference in the old university town of Lund, "Canada and the Nordic countries: Making Connections and Forging Identities." He was sure I would have some pithy things to say about that fashionable topic of the '80s: the emergence of a distinctive Canadian cultural character.

I had been gradually developing a role for myself as a print and media journalist specializing in the arts. I set out for Lund eager to show off my skills as a member of my new profession. If Canadian culture needed a bit of embellishment, I would be happy to act as an aesthetic beautician. The Canadian government had begun to talk about "cultural industries," economically viable artistic endeavours that would not only be "life-enhancing" but also "labour-intensive." As for my credentials, I had been both a businessman and an artist. As it turned out, the conference was useful. I had a chance to take a good hard look at Canadian culture in the unsparing light of a Nordic August, to eye the contrast between Canadian and Swedish artistic life, and to contrast Canada's brash, freewheeling improvisation with a deeply rooted tradition that married formality with intensity.

The conference in Lund began with an opening night banquet that happened to coincide with the beginning of the crayfish season. The convoluted compliments and somewhat heavy humour of the opening speeches fairly quickly accelerated into an unbridled celebration. The Swedes were soon devouring juicy crustaceans in an enormous quantity. Apparently the bulk of the crayfish eaten every summer in Sweden so far exceeds the local supply that they are mostly imported from Louisiana. The Swedes, however, are quite capable of producing the equally impressive amount of *aquavit* used to wash the crayfish down, so the local merchants and manufacturers still benefit from this midsummer rite. In austere and moralistic Scandinavia as elsewhere, economic gain helps preserve tribal rituals that might otherwise disappear. While we consumed, songs were sung: sentimental ballads alternating with brief scatological catches, leading to a rafter-shattering six-part rendition of "Gaudeamus Igitur."

We visiting Canadians did our best to match our hosts, tune for tune, crayfish for crayfish, glass for glass. If the shades of the Vikings who first discovered our northern shores were looking down from Valhalla, I don't think they could have disparaged the Canadians' capacity for either descant or devouring. I couldn't help contrasting the full-blooded vigour of Swedish professional revels with the self-conscious timidity of Toronto's academic jollifications. We tend to leave unrestrained licence to undergraduates; in Sweden it seems that the lines of decorum run up from the bottom rather than down from the top. That first evening in Lund, as I made my way home, stumbling uncertainly over the cobblestones behind Judy, I was stopped by a solemn youth who admonished me, concluding his lecture with what was obviously intended as the ultimate rebuke. "You will not be able to make your woman happy."

The next morning a good many of us were distinctly hung over, but we turned up dutifully for the opening address. We listened politely while an ancient Norwegian mariner recounted in carefully chosen Edwardian phrases his experiences as an explorer among the treacherous, shifting ice floes of the Canadian Arctic in the early years of the twentieth century. The privation and uncertainty he and his sailors had experienced was so dimmed by his courtly manner and formal diction that it was rather like watching a very old reel of film in which the moving shadows are barely recognizable as human figures. Eventually he concluded his account and we adjourned for a badly needed coffee break.

Then the serious academics got going. I decided to forgo three leaden-sounding papers that were simultaneously available in different lecture halls in favour of a round-table discussion with a McLuhanite flavour: "The Media and the Mystery of the Canadian Mentality." My decision was influenced in part by the fact that the session was presided over by Heidi van Born, whom Tom had tipped as a truly original personality, definitely not to be missed.

I was not disappointed. Heidi van Born turned out to be an eccentric Valkyrie with an unruly crown of defiantly dyed hair and an unexpected but telling turn of phrase, accented by the syncopated jingling of earrings and bracelets. A literary diviner, sort of a cross between Lady Ottoline Morrell and Madame Lily Tomlin, she had for nearly a decade set herself up as a tireless promoter of Canadian literature in Scandinavia; the previous year she had triumphed by welcoming to Sweden both Robertson Davies and Margaret Atwood. Now, for the Lund conference, she had lined up a bevy of somewhat lesser Canadian authors and scholars whose debates she would choreograph with considerable shrewdness, the better to lay bare the shape of our budding artistic psyche.

Heidi's welcoming preamble seemed almost deliberately erratic. She invoked "our vast immoral wastelands" and "deepening sense of unconsciousness." Did she know what she was saying? I couldn't be sure. She introduced a plump, hearty woman in a double-breasted pinstripe suit with an unmistakably Texan accent who advanced the theory that CBC Radio was the true voice of Canada, unfettered as it was by the need to make itself commercially viable by imitating American models, so that it was free to explore "ever-surprising aspects of daily reality." A lean pipe-smoker in much-patched tweed that complemented his Aberdeen brogue offered the insight that our National Film Board had concentrated on documentaries and animated cartoons, thus disposing Canadians to artistic forms of both gritty naturalism and satiric fantasy. A dog-faced woman countered in cadences edged with a distinctly German locution that the newly emerging voice of contemporary Canada could best be caught in the sharp, hiply worded lyrics and almost tuneless songs of such modern troubadours as Leonard Cohen, Joni Mitchell, and Nancy White.

These three strands were then shuttled back and forth to form a kind of tapestry of the Canadian arts scene. Various nimble-witted scholars warped and woofed, their voices gurgling with delight at their own inventiveness. We were told that the distinctive voice of Robertson Davies could only have been developed in the age of radio; Joni Mitchell was obviously influenced, if only subliminally, by Inuit throat singers; Leonard Cohen was the visual counterpart of Norman McLaren; Michael Ondaatje's prose style could be seen as a literary extension of the imagery of *The Loon's Necklace*. And so on. And on.

Just before noon, Barry Callaghan rose to his feet. "I'd like to say that I think everything we've heard here this morning is a crock. Joni Mitchell would sing like she sings even if there weren't any Eskimos. Rob Davies would be a plummy-voiced dandy if radio had never been invented. What gets me is why the Canadian government subsidizes you guys to travel three thousand miles to spew out all this malarkey instead of giving me enough dough to publish a few really promising young poets. Who is all this guff supposed to benefit anyway?"

Heidi smiled gleefully and neatly concluded the session, pointing out that Barry was scheduled to speak the next morning. He had not yet decided on a title, so she would propose one: "The Canadian Muse: Madonna, Whore, or Good Old Girl?" She beseeched us to prepare our questions and ripostes to challenge him at the question period after his address. I hurried to the front of the room to congratulate Barry on his deflationary skills. Heidi invited both of us to lunch. We adjourned to a restaurant Barry suggested. Knowing Barry, I was not surprised when Heidi exclaimed, "But this is the most extravagant eating in Lund." We drank Alsatian hock and ate a variety of smoked fish. Heidi's voice rang out across the snow-white linen of the luncheon table.

"Thank you, Barry, for starting the snowball down the mountain. Now we can all roll happily together. But no doubt you have made for yourself some enemies. You do not care?"

"He can't resist sticking pins in academics' falsies," smiled Barry's wife, Claire.

"What are these falsies? Are they like the whoopee cushion?"

"Sort of. They're both a joke. But falsies are meant to be taken seriously."

"The serious joke? But this is very much Canadian, no?"

"Exposure of fraud is vital in the arts right at the moment. The girls — and boys — with falsies are taking over the scene. Bureaucrats. Theory-spinners. Cultural carpet-baggers. They're not interested in art. They just want to line their pockets and get their faces on the TV screen. It's a damn sight easier to politicize art than to create it."

"But in the process they also promote the art, no?"

"Art isn't a popularity contest. It's nice for Little Miss Atwood that when she comes to Stockholm a whole truckload of feminists comes to the airport to greet her, but that doesn't make her write more imaginatively or even significantly. On the contrary, it will influence her to write what her editors tell her her public wants. Peggy's a strong-minded girl, but can she hold out against the image she and her publishers have created for her? I guess we'll find out."

As Barry talked about literary images, I saw in my mind's eye his father Morley: tough, outspoken, irascible. But whereas Morley came across as a little guy with no pretensions to grandeur, Barry affected a certain sweep and panache. Gourmet and gambler, tippler and tastemaker, he had the temerity to publish at his own expense not only his own work, but that of his friends and protégés. He also translated the work of foreign poets he admired: French, Polish, Irish, and Israeli. Instead of joining the ever-lengthening queues at the doors of the arts councils, he'd become a cultural entrepreneur in his own right. Not surprisingly, the pooh-bahs resented him and tried to squelch him by cutting him off from government funding. They failed to realize that their envy merely fuelled his ego. Barry lives to do battle and thrives on antagonism.

By the time lunch was over, I was too woozy to go back to the seminar room. I confided to Heidi that I didn't want my principal contribution to her conference to be the sonority of my snores. She suggested we take the afternoon off, skipping such promising topics as "The Cul-de-Sac of Canadian Post-Modernism" and "A Comparison of the Consumption and Taxation of Alcoholic Beverages in Canada and Scandinavia" to see something of Lund. She would come with us.

We walked around the town savouring the university's mélange of architectural styles spread out among manicured lawns and well-tended gardens. I thought this must have been what Cambridge and Heidelberg were like before the tourist industry got to them. The ancient cathedral was vast and spare, its soaring arches defining the space of a lofty interior uncluttered by fussy baroque tombs or swooning Mannerist statuary. The Swedish fascination with machinery and method had found expression in the cathedral's huge sixteenth-century clock, whose broad painted face showed not just the hours, but the days of the year and the phases of the moon. The calendar of saints' days was limned alongside the signs of the zodiac. Every day at three in the afternoon, the clock chimed and a procession of wise men bowed woodenly to the Virgin while, above, two armoured knights executed a series of mechanical manoeuvres with lances and battle-axes. Something for everyone, and all stunningly coordinated. I couldn't help noticing the clock's daily performances attracted a noticeably larger crowd than did the quiet fervour of the superbly sung evensong.

In the crypt we found a statue of the local giant who, legend has it, helped build the church. He was clasping a pillar in a mighty attempt to pull it down and topple the building; apparently he was denied what he believed was his just fee. "The story is much Swedish," said Heidi van Born. "The attempt to deal with powerful forces in our pagan past, the hard bargain, the frustration when we do not get the dark wishes of our heart."

Heidi proved an excellent guide to Lund, explaining everything from arcane architectural detail to current student attitudes. "Today's young are more conservative than their parents. Can you imagine, there was a riot when the university authorities wished to cut down a tree planted two hundred years ago by Linnaeus. You know, of course, who is Linnaeus. He has invented the sex life for plants."

The next day we played hooky again when Heidi promised to gain us access to the university museum, which is normally open to the public for only an hour and a half, two days a week. ("But I will speak to the director. He is my mother's cousin and also a former lover.") We spent the morning browsing through the galleries, attended by a student, shy and diffident with the uncertain promise of a beard, but fluent in English and possessing a detailed knowledge of every serene Madonna and agonized, crucified Christ on display. These figures evoked a depth of emotion that seemed to derive from the melancholy solitude of dark forests, the loneliness of long winter nights. More than the intricate intellectual footwork of the academics, the haunting presence of these early Swedish icons suggested a northern sensibility I could connect with, a community of peoples shaped by an overwhelming sense of space and a need to pursue an individual struggle against impersonal elemental forces.

In the afternoon we rented a car and drove through the southernmost province of Sweden. Skåne was once part of Denmark, and its inhabitants still speak a dialect that strongly reflects the Danish idiom. The land is fertile and highly cultivated, dotted with pretty little towns and small, well-tended castles. Heidi had explained the grounds of these houses would be open to us because Swedish law guarantees the right of access to everyone. No one would object if we spread a picnic cloth beside their pond, provided that, like responsible Swedes, we cleared up our debris before we left.

In Skåne the possibility of spontaneous discovery seemed still to exist. Every landmark was not surrounded by a ring of tourist buses disgorging hordes of avidly curious gnomes and panting behemoths struggling with cameras and walkers. We drove down dirt roads to see what we could find. A few of the Skåne castles had been converted into museums — we stopped at one called Svaneholm to view a motley collection of curiosities ranging from period furniture to a boneshaker bicycle, as well as old hay rakes and intricate bits of peasant embroidery — but most seemed to still be private houses; we were refused entry to one by a bailiff who apologized but explained they were breeding the dogs that day.

Further down the road we stopped to admire the mellow brick of a sixteenth-century manor house and talked with the gardener, who discoursed knowledgably about the cultivation of roses and eventually invited us to take tea with him. When he led us into an exquisite salon furnished with delicate rococo chairs and cabinets painted green and silver, we realized he must be the owner. He told us the furniture had been made for his great-great-grandfather by a famous French cabinetmaker whose name he had unfortunately forgotten.

We had intended to be back for Barry's lecture, but by the time we arrived he was answering questions. Barry was in his element: his big face was beaming as he confronted his hearers. He bristled like a boar, snorted like a stallion. He seemed less concerned with winning than with putting up a good fight, a pugilist giving the paying customers a good show for their money. "My generation's been lucky. We had good times and we've been able to get a few things going. I hope it will last, but I'm not counting on it. Gulley Jimson said, 'Culture follows Cash.' There may be some truth in that. But culture isn't just cash. Cash is always welcome but it leads to corruption. And corruption has to be resisted. That's what stimulates real artists. Corruption contributes to culture. Culture is conflict."

As these words were ringing in our ears, the conference ended. We sat across from Barry and Claire at the final dinner and toasted our hosts, and our country, and art, and each other, and the evening ended in a fine blur of enthusiasm and conviviality. We made plans to connect with Barry and Claire in Stockholm the next week at the *vernissage* of a show of Claire's drawings. The next morning I felt a bit guilty. I had shortchanged the great Canadian Cultural Debate, but it had been put to bed with a rousing roar from Barry, and we were free for the next week to explore Sweden.

We flew to the island of Gotland, off the southeast coast of the mainland. Just as there are civilizations which take their colour from the Mediterranean, the Caribbean, and the Pacific, so here we realized we were at the centre of an unfamiliar Baltic world with a special character of its own. Gotland has changed hands many times over the centuries and bears traces of Danish and German occupation, as well as Finnish, Polish, and Russian pirates and raiders. Yet it has remained a simple, peaceful place, truly idyllic. Its fields in late summer are a riot of wildflowers: purple vetch, pink clover, blue chicory, yellow dandelions, scarlet poppies, white daisies. There are meadows there that have never been mowed by machine. Sentimental Swedish patriots come from the mainland cities during the holidays and clear the fields by hand with sickles and scythes.

Gotland is not a land of monuments but of cultural memories, for the Swedes a reminder of a simpler, cleaner past — a notion a North American finds it easy to connect with. As a Canadian in Europe, I've never missed the roar and bustle of thronging cities; rather, I've longed for the open space of our wilderness (even though I've spent little enough time in it). In Gotland, that sense of space is still potent. We drove through tall, forbidding pinewoods expecting to see trolls at every turning, and explored tiny villages, usually just a few houses and a church with the tall conical spire typical of the island. These churches were open every day, untended except for an occasional gravedigger, who would look up slowly, nod solemnly, and then go back to work.

Each church had its own treasure: fancifully carved and painted pews depicting the women of the Bible from Sarah to Salome, a huge painted dragon curling up over beams and rafters to spew fire at an uneasy St. George crouched in a corner of the apse or in the tiny southern church of Öja, a *Mater Dolorosa* whose grief was infinitely moving because it seemed utterly and intensely private.

This was not castle country, though there were a few fine villas, mostly built by artists, including the studio-workshop of Canadian impressionist William Blair Bruce, whose Swedish wife persuaded him to settle on the south shore near the walled city of Visby at the turn of the twentieth century. His house, Brucebo, contained some of his paintings. Others had been sold off to provide funding so that every year a Canadian artist could be sent to study in Europe. Further along the same shore we discovered a grander villa that seemed deserted. Its formal gardens were full of Milles-like sculptures, its rooms decorated in a style that suggested Matisse, but more nervous, more self-conscious: attenuated Pans piping, fauns nervously fondling skinny nymphets. A celebration of paganism whose inspiration owed more to Strindberg than Homer.

Strindberg and Bergman: the two master spirits whose vision shaped the image of Sweden, at least in my mind. I knew the northern tip of Gotland was Bergman country; many of his movies were shot there and he still maintained an isolated retreat on a small private island off the shores of Fårö. We drove there hoping for a glimpse of the famous filmmaker, disregarding a warning that foreigners were banned from this area, which is the site of strategic military manoeuvres. We were easily able to penetrate the security system of the Swedish army but not that of the guardians of Bergman's privacy.

I walked along the pebbly shore and looked longingly across at his haven. Shrieking seabirds flew overhead, and also whining triads of triangular jets. I was accosted by a solitary sunbather, an aging nude Fricka with huge, bouncing bare breasts and grey locks streaming in the breeze. "So you would see the great Bergman. Impossible. He vants only to be alone." I savoured the echo of Garbo; could it have been unconscious?

Two days later, back in Stockholm, I was received by the artistic director of the Kungliga Dramatiska Teatern, where Bergman was still staging theatrical productions. We stood in the lobby drinking champagne under a rich and fanciful ceiling mural painted by Carl Larsen: more bare gods and goddesses flaunting their golden charms, well beyond our reach. Polite compliments were exchanged before I adjourned to a bar across the street with Stellan Skarsgård, an intense blond actor, acknowledged as the most notable Scandinavian Hamlet of his generation. "Bergman is a magician," he told me. "Also a devil. He promises to lead you to truth, but he wants complete control of your life. He tells you to give up drinking, to leave your wife. I have been enough under his thumb. Here in Sweden we are all too much in awe of authority. I must leave this company. Anyway, I cannot work here now they have added 'Royal' to our name."

Stellan Skarsgård talked about a film he had made in Alberta. "In Canada, you have so much the possibility. I loved pretending to be a cowboy, but working conditions were not so good. We had a Czech director, an Italian cameraman, French and Swedish actors. Stimulating. But in every shot there were young girls wiggling and squirming. So I asked the director, 'What has this to do with the story?' He replied, 'Please, I cannot concentrate with all these questions.' The next day he was gone. Fired from the set. I do not think Canadian film is yet very serious."

I made a point of catching a Swedish film in which Stellan Skarsgård played a landlord who, when his tenant cannot pay the rent, insists on sleeping with his wife. Eventually the tenant, in a fit of jealous rage, cuts off the landlord's penis and throws it in the fire. Soon after, the entire cast is killed in an avalanche. I couldn't help wondering if this is what the Swedes meant by serious.

The spirit of Bergman also led me to Drottningholm; he designed his film of Mozart's *Magic Flute* to be shot in its eighteenth-century theatre. (I learned when I got there that the camera equipment proved too heavy for the ancient floors and a studio set simulating the Drottningholm theatre had to be built in a Stockholm warehouse.) The theatre is magical the way Bergman's early movies are; it conjures up ghosts of another age. In its tiny auditorium the lights were dim and flickering like candles; it prevents the fabrics from fading and discourages visitors from realizing that the decoration is mostly *trompe-l'oeil*, and rather roughly sketched in at that. The grandeur of the lobby is as much an illusion as the rolling waves and receding colonnades onstage. The theatre then, as now, was hard up.

Under the stage we explored a world of ropes and pulleys, capstans and hatches. A pretty young theatre historian explained to me that the whole edifice had been designed by a master shipbuilder. "The sailor must improvise with limited means to create the illusion of a life in which there is space and comfort. The craft and precision of the seaman surpasses that of the landsman in economy and elegance." In this theatre order and ingenuity were used to produce wonder and delight, charming the audience not into belief, but into the willing suspension of criticism.

Drottningholm's theatre is a lovingly maintained relic of the past where performances are still given regularly. The Palace itself was also still in use, the preferred home of Sweden's King, Carl Gustaf, and Queen Silvia and their three children. We saw him walking down towards the lake with his wife, carrying a tennis racket and a duffle bag. He came across as a typical country gentleman with a passion for sport. She was a Brazilian beauty, and her combination of personal magnetism and shrewd management have been credited by many with having preserved the monarchy of probably the most socialistic state west of the Soviet Union.

We were told that the royal children went to the local public school. The eldest, Princess Victoria, will inherit the throne, even though she has a younger brother. In keeping with contemporary notions of equality, the laws of succession have been changed and the eldest child becomes monarch, regardless of sex (perhaps the royalists have picked up on the considerable clout that female royals seemed to have in respect to their masculine consorts. England's Diana, Monaco's Stéphanie, Spain's Sofía, and even Holland's Beatrix command instant recognition, but who remembers the features of Olaf of Norway or Baudouin of Belgium?).

Drottningholm, like so many buildings in Sweden, has a human scale. It is Versailles in miniature; its formal gardens don't seem to stretch out to infinity but lead to a pleasant prospect of wheat fields and birch woods. The grounds contain a delicate Chinese pavilion, whose playful elegance makes the splendours of Brighton and Schönbrunn seem vulgar and overstated. The original decorations in Delft blue, terracotta, and apple green are still intact and show off a unique collection of porcelain chinoiserie figures: mandarins and monkeys and graceful ladies hiding behind their fans. The pavilion is used for special royal parties, small state dinners, and the birthdays of the princesses.

The spirit of the eighteenth century is so strong at Drottningholm, it was easy to fantasize that the royal family must still wear panniers and perruques. But the claim of modernity was asserted by the king's sleek, white launch moored at the palace steps; we saw him jump aboard and take the wheel himself so he could zip down to Stockholm to attend some state function. Did he have his crown stowed in his duffle bag or just some herring sandwiches run up by Queen Silvia for him to munch on the way? In any case, he turned with a bright smile and waved to her with his free hand as he steered his trim little craft out into the open sea.

Stockholm's centre also retains an eighteenth-century character — a sense of proportion and decorum, the buildings rich but not lavish, ornamented but not ostentatious. The central island of the old city is compact, workable, and full of quiet, ongoing life. Tugboats pull barges piled with beer barrels past the splendour of the Riddarholmen cathedral, where kings and heroes lie buried. Old men fish for salmon a foot away from the white-helmeted sentinels in front of the royal palace. In the evening people stroll along the Västerlånggatan and listen to the buskers, but by eleven the streets are empty.

Except on Saturday night when high-spirited youths roam through the streets of the Old Town singing and spewing till well after midnight. They weave in and out of tiny half-hidden bars and basement dance halls, where live musicians offer everything from expertly counterfeited '50s jazz to a sort of Scandinavian rockabilly. I was tipped off about a nightclub too naughty to be mentioned in the guidebooks, and found it with some difficulty. It offered an old-fashioned drag show featuring a magician in high heels and false eyelashes, the sort of act that might have appeared at a second-class Miami nightclub in the mid-'50s, complete with rednecks yelling insults and the performers responding with bitchy putdowns.

Early Sunday morning proved to be the best time to savour Stockholm, to walk from the Old Town, around the harbour, and into the royal park of Skansen. Here are many fine houses built in the early twentieth century by inventive architects who picked up on the spirit of the *jugendstil* and married it to the detail of ancient Norse carvings to produce a distinctive Nordic revival style that found its ultimate expression in the soaring city hall with its glittering gold and blue mosaics. The building provides a fitting setting for state balls and Nobel banquets, but it is also rented out for visiting conventions and private functions; I was assured by the proud guide that it has been a big money-maker for the city fathers who built it.

The villas of Skansen and the superb examples of early twentieth-century glass and furniture in the National Museum explain where modern Scandinavian design came from. It is part of an ongoing process, an exploration of craftsmanship, driven by the desire to marry fantasy and practicality, invention and tradition, to create new forms that are striking in their strength and simplicity.

My musings on the origins of modern Swedish design were broken by the appearance of a man with a fiercely wasted face. He looked as though he had crammed fifty years of experience into thirty. He asked for a cigarette and I thought, "Aha, a Swedish bum." But I had no tobacco and he was not interested when I offered him money. He showed me a nasty flesh wound, which he claimed was the result of a skirmish with the police when he had tried to come to the rescue of a black man who insisted on dancing in the street after the police had told him to move along. He denounced the soul-destroying power of modern bureaucracy. He would leave Sweden soon to find some place where the individual was still respected. Not in Europe: the Danish were only interested in a good time, the Germans were too stuck up, the Italians were all whores. Possibly Canada. What were the prospects for him there? I started to explain the point system used by Canadian immigration officials and he threw me a withering look. He took a bottle of *aquavit* from his pocket, swallowed a healthy draught, handed me the heel of the bottle, and lay down on a park bench. In a matter of seconds he was snoring loudly.

That afternoon we drove to Gripsholm with the Delworths. Older than Drottningholm, its towers, dungeons, portraits, and pickaxes evoke the history of the kings and queens of Sweden, who count among their number some vivid personalities: Gustaf III, the enlightened autocrat whose assassination provided Verdi with the plot for his opera *Un Ballo in Maschera*; Queen Christina, a sort of Swedish counterpart of Mary, Queen of Scots, who inspired one of Greta Garbo's most luminous performances; Jean-Baptiste Bernadotte, the French Marshal chosen to be King of Sweden, who turned on his former emperor when he discovered he had been the lover of his beautiful wife

Désirée (thus providing the plot for a bestselling novel and giving Marlon Brando an opportunity to impersonate Napoleon).

Tom Delworth explained that he was currently trying to line up a visit to Canada by the King and Queen, who first met at the Olympics in Munich in the early '70s and had since, whenever possible, attended the games, supporting sport with a splash of sentiment. They had expressed an interest in visiting Calgary, and the word had reached Tom. He thought it might be a popular gesture to invite the couple to make a state visit. But our government, with typical Canadian caution, did not wish to initiate a formal overture until they were sure Carl Gustaf and Silvia would accept; they, with characteristic Swedish reserve, were unwilling to discuss the matter until they received an official invitation. Things seemed to have reached an impasse; after six months of tactfully phrased innuendo and delicately dropped hints, no direct communication had taken place. But Tom was sanguine. "Nothing is done in a hurry here. Everything is deliberated by a committee democratically constituted and conducted according to established precedent. Changes can be made, but only after they have been thoroughly weighed, and all the implications considered. And then you can be sure they won't be changed back in a hurry. That's what makes Sweden one of the most advanced and, at the same time, one of the most traditional countries in the world."

"You think Canadians can take some pointers from the Swedes?"

"We have a lot in common. Northern reserve, scepticism. A willingness to let things find their own shape."

"But aren't we trying to force Canadian culture to develop? Legislate it into existence?"

"A little forcing can be a good thing. The Swedes may be reserved but they're not passive. They're tough and determined and autocratic." I thought of Bergman. And the bum.

The next day, a fresh contingent of Canadian cultural grandees, among them Harbourfront's Greg Gatenby and McClelland & Stewart's Adrienne Clarkson, arrived at the embassy. They'd been attending the Gothenburg Book Fair, one of Europe's major literary events. For four days they'd been trading bons mots and barbs with international best-selling writers: Britain's crime queen P.D. James and existentialist novelist Iris Murdoch, France's political philosopher Bernard-Henri Lévy, Russia's controversial critic Valentin Rasputin, Latin America's revolutionary priest Ernesto Cardenal, America's prolific sexual chronicler John Updike, and popular healer of battered psyches Dr. Ruth.

Tom and his wife, Pamela, gave a literary reception for Clarkson and Gatenby, who appeared utterly unfazed after their brush with so much literary eminence. They worked their way through the roomful of Swedish literati like true professionals, buoyed by the knowledge that both had cut deals and were on their way home with prizes in their pockets: Clarkson would introduce Canadian readers to the works of Swedish novelist Sven Delblanc, who happened to have been born in Manitoba; Gatenby had helped broker an invitation for Heidi von Born to spend a year visiting the University of Victoria. The party also honoured Barry and Claire, whose show was to open the following afternoon.

After the Swedes departed, we sat on the veranda of the pretty Nordic revival house that serves as the Canadian residence. (It was built by the Swedish inventor Gustaf Dalén, who developed, among other things, the automatic lighthouse and the AGA stove.) We gossiped about friends and foes at home as we looked across the sound at the sun setting behind the fairy-tale towers and domes of Stockholm's skyline. Adrienne Clarkson recalled that she had been Tom's guest years before when she was a travelling student and he was in Sweden as a fledgling diplomat on his first posting abroad. Now the theme of a Canadian-Swedish parallel had resurfaced.

"I knew then that I'd be coming back here. There's much we Canadians can learn here. The spirit of this country is not only challenging but also very convincing. It has something to do with scale but also independence of mind."

"But we're creating a very different sort of society in Canada." I posited. "We're never going to be a country like France or Sweden with two thousand years of tradition and the homogeneity provided by a shared language and racial heritage."

"We can certainly learn something by choosing a first-rate model. The Swedes have been willing to pay the price of their independence. They've been able to control their own destiny, and at the same time create a model of what a northern country can be."

The next day Clarkson and Gatenby departed. Judy and I turned up early for Claire's opening at a fashionable little downtown gallery with Tom. There was white wine and smoked fish and subdued chatter. The drawings were lush, sensuous, and unashamedly erotic. It was clear that Tom was not comfortable with this panoply of breasts and penises. "Deftly done, but frankly not exactly my taste," he demurred. We went to where Claire stood at the end of the gallery, smiling mischievously. Tom complimented her on her draughtsmanship and her smile broadened. He made his excuses and slipped away.

A few minutes later Heidi von Born made her entrance in a green velvet cloak that might have graced the shoulders of Isolde setting out for Cornwall. She made a sweeping tour of the drawings, then turned to Claire. "My dear, I can see why you so disdain the falsies."

"We had our share of them last night at the embassy. And I have to say Stockholm can match Toronto phony for phony."

Barry filled our glasses with Dom Pérignon, which I knew he must have provided himself.

"Then I must, in Canada, watch where I am to be stepping."

I raised my glass to toast Heidi. "You'll do fine in Canada. I can tell you're a tough nut."

"I am the nut who is tough to crack. Perhaps this is something what you can learn from we Swedes. To be a little more tough."

"You're more than just tough. You have strong instincts."

"Ah, the instincts. Always I follow them, and now they lead me into the wilderness. But you are right. I survive. Is that not the message of your Margaret Atwood?"

Barry chuckled. "Smart girl, our Peggy. She hit the nail on the head. We've got used to good times and we keep imagining they will go on getting better. But I don't think so. The name of the game for all of us in the next twenty years is going to be just that. Survival."

RADIO DAYS

Like many of the brightest students at the Drama Centre, Damiano Pietropaolo made his way through the coursework required to obtain a Ph.D. but got stuck before he completed his thesis. My belief is that most graduate students spend many hours in the library assembling a vast collection of facts, both relevant and irrelevant, about their chosen topic, then find themselves at a loss as to how this mountain of information might be shaped into a coherent whole. When I started to work seriously as a writer, I decided to follow a different pattern. I would read one or two articles and perhaps interview three people. I would then write a first draft, which would show me which holes needed plugging, thus avoiding hours of unproductive research. This served me well in my work as a journalist and would turn out to be even more important as my work expanded into a related field.

Damiano, who had a wife and three children to support, found work in radio at the CBC, which in the late '80s and '90s still provided an outlet for the talents of a group of imaginative and intelligent people whose work was enjoyed by a select but fairly widespread audience. Damiano became a protégé of Geraldine Sherman, the wife of Robert Fulford, and a demanding, indeed rigorous, producer/editor of the program *Ideas*, which, as its name suggests, dealt with complex and stimulating topics demanding close attention and mental alertness from its listeners.

One day I was having lunch with Damiano at Dooney's, a bistro on Bloor Street West, which was a hangout for older Italian men but also a number of more or less left-wing intellectual types such as Rick Salutin and Howard Engel. Damiano suggested I should try my hand at writing for radio and challenged me to come up with a topic for a program on *Ideas*. After a couple of suggestions that failed to pique his interest, I came up with a proposal to do a piece on John Glassco, whose *Memoirs of Montparnasse* I had recently read. Damiano was interested in the ambience of Paris in the '20s and he succeeded in selling the idea to Geraldine.

I busied myself re-reading the *Memoirs* and also Glassco's poetry, which, although not widely known, had won him a Governor General's Award, and also several of his pornographic novels, written under a pseudonym. I decided that bits of the *Memoirs* could be dramatized. I recorded interviews with his editor, William Toye; his widow Marion, who was still living in Montreal in the house she and her husband had shared; the distinguished critic Leon Edel, who had known Glassco at the end of his life in Hawaii; Margaret Atwood, who as an aspiring young poet had sought him out in Montreal; and most enlightening of all, his rival Morley Callaghan, who was still living in an old house in Rosedale and whom I often met in the neighbourhood grocery store.

Callaghan and Glassco had taken an instant dislike to each other; Callaghan had written a satirical short story about Glassco and his friend, Graeme Taylor, in which he hinted that they were lovers, and Glassco wrote disparagingly about Callaghan in the *Memoirs*. In his interview, Callaghan was appropriately vinegary; Edel gave an astute evaluation of Glassco's poetry; Atwood contributed a wry remembrance of his gallantry towards her in her youth; but the most interesting revelation came from a young student in Montreal who had managed to gain access to some of Glassco's papers. Glassco had claimed that the memoir was written in the '20s just after he came home from Paris. But, in fact, the manuscript was written in ballpoint, which proved that it in fact had been written some thirty years later. This was news to his editor, as was the fact that the book was part reminiscence, part invention.

I dramatized a few scenes from the book, which was easy to do because Glassco had written some very sharp and lively dialogue. We hired Richard Monette to play the young Glassco, or Buffy, as he was known to his contemporaries, and also to read some of the poems. To play the American femme fatale Honour Quayle, we engaged Jackie Burroughs, who had played Ophelia opposite Richard's Hamlet at the Crest Theatre when Richard was only nineteen. Richard recalled that in rehearsals Jackie had cried a lot and asked if she intended to do the same before we went into the studio. Jackie replied that she thought that was an excellent idea and headed into the ladies' washroom, handkerchief in hand. She returned a few minutes later and said to me, "Now tell me about this woman. Not that anything you say will have the slightest influence on my interpretation." In fact, she was perfect as the man-devouring seductress and Richard, who was an accomplished mimic, was able to give a very accurate impression of Glassco, whose voice we were able find reading one of his poems for an earlier CBC broadcast.

The two-part series was well received and indeed was rebroadcast twice.

Although my initial fee was not princely, I received an additional fee every time it reappeared, so in the end I was reasonably well paid for my labour. The broadcast also did something to revive interest in Glassco and particularly the *Memoir*. Bill Toye was keen to sell the film rights in order to provide some income for Glassco's widow Marion. He sent a young man to see me, who wanted to option the property and claimed to have backers. He offered me a chance to write the screenplay. Bill asked me for my opinion of him, and I said he seemed both persuasive and aggressive, which I thought augured well for his future as a film producer. He was exposed soon after as a thief; he disappeared, and so did any immediate prospect of a film.

I took the idea to Dick Nielsen, who at the time had just had a considerable success with the CBC series *The Newcomers*. He expressed mild interest. Shortly thereafter I mentioned the project to Adrienne Clarkson when I visited her in Paris, where she was functioning as Ontario Agent-General. She told me she thought the piece unsuitable for filming. About a year later, I learned that Adrienne had taken out an option for the film rights. She and her partner, John Ralston Saul, were planning to set up a film production company. However, she accepted a position as publisher with McClelland & Stewart and her ambitions as a filmmaker languished. A few years later Dick Nielsen got in touch with me and gave me a stage version of the *Memoirs* that he had written. I did not think it a very skilful adaptation and, as it involved a huge cast, it seemed impractical for the only kind of production I might have been able to negotiate for him.

Still later, I was approached by Berthold Carrière when he was music director at Stratford. He was looking for a book and lyrics for a musical for which he could compose the music. I set to work on a treatment and sent it to him. I heard nothing for some time, which I have learned in the theatre is not a good sign. No news is definitely *not* good news. He eventually managed to convey to me that it was not what he was looking for. I thought of approaching my sometime-collaborator John Roby, but learned that he was already working on a similar story with another writer. Though my efforts to dramatize the *Memoirs* came to nothing, the book would resurface later in another context.

My next venture for *Ideas* was three programs on the life and work of Robertson Davies under the title "Demons and Delights." I spent several mornings with Davies in his office, and he gave me very detailed information about his experiences and theories: the importance of various figures in his life, most notably his own father, Senator Rupert Davies; the renowned British director Tyrone Guthrie, whom he called his "father in art"; and the Canadian diplomat and philanthropist Vincent Massey, who fingered him to be the first master of Massey College. He told many amusing and revelatory anecdotes about all of these men and about his method of working. I interviewed his biographer, Judith Skelton Grant; the critic Robert Fulford; British novelist Margaret Drabble; my brother-in-law, James Cunningham, who had stayed with the Davies family as a teenager; and the drama critic Ronald Bryden. All of them were admirers, though some of them included sharp comments. I also interviewed one or two academics, but their comments were on the whole so dull that I decided not to use them.

I interviewed Davies' surviving brother, Arthur, and his daughter Miranda, who told some interesting stories of her childhood and then decided she didn't want me to use them.

Robertson's wife, Brenda, declined to be interviewed until Rob spoke to her, and she then contributed some amusing detail about the time when they were both employed by Guthrie at the Old Vic, and their subsequent ocean voyage to Canada in the early days of the Second World War.

I lifted short scenes from some of Davies' plays, dramatized parts of the novels, and even included one of the Massey College ghost stories, which Davies famously delivered every December at the Massey College Gaudy Night. I was fortunate in getting some excellent actors, among them Barbara Chilcott, Nicky Guadagni, and Douglas Campbell. But the actor who made the most vital contribution was Angelo Rizacos. Like other actors I would work with in radio, notably Richard Monette and Stephen Ouimette, his vocal control was impressive and he could fit a speech to accompanying music, or shave twenty seconds off a speech on demand. He also had a wonderful quality of wondering innocence, which, although it hardly seemed synonymous with Davies' mature persona, perfectly suited some of the younger characters in his work. I came to appreciate how skilled some of the actors who worked in radio in those days were, even though they often worked for a pittance.

The programs benefited greatly from the inclusion of a variety of types of music, much of it chosen in consultation with Davies. The interweaving of the music with the text was accomplished by a highly skilled technician who had worked extensively with Glenn Gould. Davies expressed himself delighted with the finished product, and it was repeated a year or two later. The chief producer of *Ideas*, Bernie Lucht, promised it would be repeated again when Davies died. As it turned out, I was in Mexico when this happened. I sent a message to Bernie Lucht, but by this time I was no longer a regular contributor to *Ideas* and the rebroadcast didn't happen. I am happy that I was able to give this tribute to Davies, who had always been supportive of my work and had a major influence on my career.

About this time, Eleanor Wachtel began her program interviewing authors, and she apparently let it be known to the *Ideas* producers that they were not to do any programs about literary figures, as this was now her territory. Damiano suggested to me that he had wanted to do a series of programs about different types of drama: comedy, tragedy, and the mixture of both that dominated theatre in the twentieth century. We discussed this idea briefly when he informed me that he had been promoted to a full position as a drama producer. He turned me over to another producer he had worked with, Alison Moss. She was an attractive red-haired woman with a warm and receptive personality, and we got along well together.

With her guidance I developed three scripts about the different types of drama, which probably differed considerably from Damiano's original concept. The first, about comedy, was centred around an actual production of *The Taming of the Shrew* that Richard Monette directed at Stratford. We included short scenes from this production, along with interviews with Richard, as well as Colm Feore and Goldie Semple, who played the leading characters Petruchio and Katherine.

The second category, tragedy, was represented by a production of *Hedda Gabler* at the Shaw Festival, starring Fiona Reid and adapted and directed by Judith Thompson, both of whom agreed to be interviewed. These two talented and strong-minded women had somewhat different concepts of the play, and the program reflected this tension. The final episode involved a production of Michel Tremblay's *Damnée Manon, Sacrée Sandra.* I interviewed the actors Diana Leblanc and Jean-Francois Blanchard and also went to Montreal to interview Tremblay, whom I had heard could be difficult. I arrived at his apartment on the wrong day, but he proved to be hospitable, charming, and witty.

These programs drew a less enthusiastic response than the earlier ones and I thought perhaps my days with *Ideas* were over.

I made another proposal which I called "Public Convictions, Private Lives." This centred on the career of Canadian diplomat John Watkins, whom I had known as a junior foreign service officer in Ottawa, and the expulsion of a number of senior officers in the Department of External Affairs at the insistence of the CIA.

Watkins had been the Canadian ambassador to the USSR and had briefly taken up with a young homosexual lover when travelling in one of the more remote provinces of Russia. The lover, a young poet, betrayed him to the KGB, who threatened Watkins unless he co-operated with them by promoting policies which the Russians favoured. Although he agreed, there is no evidence that in fact he did so. He returned to Canada and functioned as undersecretary of the department before retiring to live in Paris. His story was brought to light by a double agent a few years later. Watkins was asked by the RCMP to return to Canada for questioning. He was met at the airport in Montreal and escorted to a motel, where he was questioned for two days before he died of a heart attack. The whole affair was hushed up at the time.

My program covered not only the story of Watkins but also his fellow officer Herbert Norman, who was hounded by United States agents who accused him of being a Communist during the McCarthy hearings. He was sent to New Zealand, where it was supposed he would not be subject to further investigation, but was then appointed ambassador to Egypt. The Americans again threatened to investigate him, and he jumped from the roof of the embassy to his death. I managed to obtain very intelligent interviews about these two men from my friends Peter Russell and Charles Taylor.

There is some reason to think that Norman also indulged in homosexual activities. I was aware of a number of other officers whom I had known who were expelled from External Affairs. It is interesting that positions of some importance were found for them. Peter Campbell became a senior bureaucrat at the CBC; John Holmes became the president of the Canadian Institute of International Affairs; Douglas LePan became president of University College. I asked him if I could interview him on this subject and he agreed on the condition that I agreed not to "out" Lester B. Pearson. Unfortunately, he died a few days later. Although I was allowed to tell the stories of Watkins and Norman in full, I was discouraged from pursuing the story of Pearson's possible involvement on the grounds of lack of evidence. I had already learned that there was a certain amount of self-censorship practiced by all the Canadian media. The standard reply to a journalist who suggested the idea of investigating some highly controversial subject was, "Our public does not want to hear this." Whether I had crossed a forbidden line or not I was not sure, but I was not commissioned to do any further programs for *Ideas*.

One day when we were working together in the editing studio, Damiano told me that he had been asked to write something Italian for *Morningside*, the show that Peter Gzowski hosted for three hours, five days a week. Gzowski had a relaxed and genial manner, which I was to learn didn't carry over into his private conversation, and was a highly skilled interviewer. His show was very popular with a wide range of people from painters and construction workers who listened to him on the job to office-workers, housewives, and invalids who heard him at home. Every day there was a dramatic segment in the program, usually in the form of a fifteen-minute episode serialized over five or even ten days.

Damiano sent me to the office of Barry Morgan, one of a stable of drama producers that included John Douglas, Stephen Katz, Bill Lane, and James Roy. I had a nodding acquaintance with all of them except Barry, but he welcomed me affably.

"I hear you have an idea for a series of programs about Italy."

I knew of course that he was hoping I could come up with something that would appeal to Toronto's large Italian community. This was in the early days of the media's interest in multiculturalism. I was completely unprepared, but knew I had to come up with something. "What about Verdi? All that wonderful music."

"I think we did something about Verdi a couple of seasons ago, didn't we?'

"Puccini then."

"Great idea. I'll have a contract drawn up and sent to you."

And that was it.

I knew virtually nothing about Puccini except that I had always loved the melodies from *La Bohème* and *Madama Butterfly*. I went to the music library at the University of Toronto and found a biography of Puccini, which I read with interest. It seemed he was a bon vivant and a great womanizer, and all his operas are about women who have problems with men. So there was my theme. All I had to do was dramatize his life story, beginning with him running off with another man's wife, and leaving room for the insertion of his greatest tunes.

I completed the draft of ten episodes in a matter of two weeks and gave it to Barry. "We only want five episodes, so select the ones that you think are most important. However, I think it will play like gangbusters."

"Thanks."

"I'm serious. We need to talk about casting."

I suggested Monette for Puccini. "He's half Italian. I named some other Italian-Canadian actors I knew, several of them from the cast of *Johnny Bananas*. Barry followed my suggestions for the most part. "You have a flair for casting. I might as well take advantage of it."

I had decided that it would be impossible to match up a whole slew of recordings of various singers, even if we could afford to pay for the rights. I wrote the script so that we heard Puccini composing at his piano. We could thus control the musical input using exactly as much or as little as we wanted. Barry was delighted with this device. "Do you think you can find someone to play the music?" I replied that I thought I could.

A few weeks later, I received a call from Barry. "Have you lined up that guy to play the piano? Can he come in tomorrow?"

"To talk about what you want him to do?'

"Hell, no. To play. We're going into the recording studio tomorrow morning."

I called my old friend Stuart Hamilton, who agreed to take on the job. "Here's the deal. You get the music. Mark the passages you want and I'll play them. I guess a few wrong notes won't matter if he's composing at the piano." In fact, Stuart was a skilled pianist who coached opera singers and masterminded Opera in Concert. I was lucky to get him.

The next day Barry, Stuart, the actors, and I gathered in the studio for an initial read-through. In spite of their ethnic background, their pronunciation of Italian was execrable and needed coaching, which I was able to provide. Monette seemed particularly ill-equipped to get his tongue around the diphthongs with which the language abounds. "I thought you told me he was half Italian," said Barry.

"I'm Italian from the waist down."

Stuart announced that he expected me to stand beside him at the piano to indicate exactly what he was to play. "I hope you read music." I was able to reply in the affirmative. "Good, then you can turn the pages for me."

The whole session went smoothly and very rapidly. I was glad I was there to correct a number of misunderstandings and make a few cuts where necessary. I would make a point of always attending recording sessions of my scripts in the future. Barry was delighted with the finished tape, and apparently the show was well received. He called me some weeks later to ask, "What next?"

"I thought maybe something Middle Eastern?"

"Do you know anything about that part of the world?"

"I recently came back from six months there."

"Oh, all right. You'd better do me a one-page outline."

I responded with the plot for a series titled *Allies*. It was roughly based on a play I had written shortly after returning from Saudi Arabia. Its central character was a Canadian diplomat stationed in an imaginary emirate in the Persian Gulf.

Graydon, the Canadian, was a witty, rather easygoing fellow who had lost his initial ambition to improve the world and found himself caught between the machinations of the wily local British ambassador and the brash young American *chargé d'affaires*. Graydon's daughter, a medical doctor, turns out to be romantically involved not only with the American, but also with a local prince. There is also a terrorist lurking in the desert. The plot was complicated but the tone was light-hearted. It was an attempt on my part to deal with the politics of the region at a time in the mid-'80s — over a decade before 9/11 — when the Western world was not yet fixated on or even much aware of what was going on in the area.

The casting was less than ideal: Graydon was played by Ron Hartmann, who had reservations about the script, which he thought facile, and he failed to capture the humour and resilience of his character; Diana Leblanc, who played his wife, saw her as something of a martyr, rather than as a wise and tolerant middle-aged woman. The girl who played the daughter, though glamorous, lacked the adventurous and daring spirit that I wanted her character to possess, and an American black man was cast as a sophisticated African-Chinese doctor. He admitted he had no knowledge of the Caribbean and no idea what his character was about. These were not the only problems. My plot was too convoluted for many listeners to follow, especially if they missed one or two parts of the series. With this outing I learned that for this particular program, each episode must have a story that can stand on its own.

On one of my frequent visits to Montreal, I was introduced by my friends Gerald Budner and Eric McLean to a recording of a Quebecois singer called

La Bolduc. I learned she had been an enormously popular folk singer who wrote her own distinctive patter songs and travelled all over French-speaking North America, which at the time included New Brunswick, Maine, Windsor, Winnipeg, and upper New York State, in her heyday in the 1920s and '30s. She is still fondly remembered in Quebec but completely unknown in English-speaking Canada. I promoted the idea of telling her story on *Morningside*, saying she was the Bessie Smith of Quebec, although in many ways she was more like Kate Smith. In time I gained the receptive ear of Stephen Katz before he succumbed to AIDS. Then I took the idea to Damiano, who had just been appointed head of radio drama and features. He found my proposal interesting but said, "You're an Anglo and a male; you'd better find yourself a Francophone female co-writer."

I went to Montreal where I met with Maureen Labonté. She seemed an ideal writing partner. Maureen did some valuable research as she had access to better source material. After a month or two I felt I had enough information to get started and I wrote the first episode, which I sent to Maureen in Montreal. I waited a month, and when I didn't hear from her I phoned her and asked if she had received my draft.

"Oh, yes."

"You didn't like it?"

"It's fine, but the thing is . . . I'm now working for Radio-Canada, the French network. I told them about our project and they said if I continued with it, they'd have to let me go."

I went back to Damiano who frowned and then said, "What the hell, you'd better finish it and give it to Dave." Dave Carley was a young playwright who had recently been hired as dramaturge for CBC Radio. Damiano told me he would have offered me the job but felt I didn't need it as badly as Dave did. Fortunately, Dave liked my script and Damiano decided to offer my project to a young up-and-coming producer, Gregory Sinclair.

Greg had acted for me at Hart House Theatre before coming to work for CBC Radio. He was a handsome and good-tempered young guy and, though not a particularly talented actor, was both intelligent and savvy. He quickly saw that the music would be crucial. I suggested we approach my friend John Roby. John agreed to arrange La Bolduc's tunes to the English lyrics I had devised and to assemble a small band. Greg insisted we needed someone with experience in music theatre and suggested we approach Louise Pitre. I had never heard of her but Greg had seen her playing the lead in *Les Misérables* and was sure she could deliver what was required. I persuaded Greg we should cast the show using all French-Canadian actors, of whom there were a considerable number in Toronto. They wouldn't be concerned with *acting* French; they would simply *be* French.

The day for the first read-through arrived. I was nervous, especially as the studio started to fill up with actors I didn't know, all speaking French. At two minutes before the appointed start time, an elegant woman with snow-white hair appeared. "Who wrote this script?" she asked.

"I did.'

"It's my mother, my aunts, my grandmother. How did you know about this?"

"Because it's my mother and my aunts. They were farmers on the Ontario side of the Ottawa River. I guess farmers are pretty much the same everywhere."

"I think it's terrific." I adored her from that moment on.

Louise gave a wonderful performance: dynamic, vital, and at the same time earthy. Not only did she have a rich and powerful voice, but she brought a ready sense of humour and a practicality to the role that was perfect for Bolduc. She had learned all the songs and easily got her tongue around the "turletages," the rapid-fire nonsense syllables with which Bolduc embellished all her choruses. The cast included a number of actors that I would get to know well and work with in the future, particularly Donald Carrier. The show was popular with Gzowski's audience, who wrote some thirty complimentary letters (including one from one of Bolduc's granddaughters), an almost unprecedented response to a morning drama.

My next effort for *Morningside* was an adaptation of five short stories by Mavis Gallant. I had met her when she was a visiting fellow at Massey College and found her to be entertaining, though highly acerbic. When I asked her for permission to adapt some of her stories, she asked which ones and was evidently pleased with my selection, although she said she would have to think about it. I believe she was more influenced by the offer of a fee than by my credentials. I found the work difficult to recast in dramatic form because of Mme Gallant's elliptical style. She would often begin with a sentence such as this: "Ordinarily Alice would not have chosen to consult with her friend Mary but in this instance she felt the need of some friendly counsel, though she continued to hold back at least to begin with." *How do you dramatize that?* I wondered. But I forged ahead.

Once again, Greg Sinclair was to be my producer but it was decided at the last moment that the taping should be done in Montreal, as that city had been Gallant's childhood home. For some reason that I no longer remember, I was unable to travel with Greg to be present at the taping. When I heard the resulting programs I was disappointed. Many of the roles seemed miscast and the programs lacked the sort of nuance that I took to be essential to the writer's work. This may have been my fault as much as Greg's, although I could not help feeling that had I been present in the studio, I would have been able to exert some influence in shaping the actors' interpretations. I decided to send a copy of the tapes to Mme Gallant in Paris. Cannily, she responded immediately with a thank-you note before she could possibly have had time to listen to them and thus didn't have to comment on the quality of the work.

I followed this up with a proposal to write a piece that was inspired by a real-life situation. Brian Johnson had been drama critic for the *Globe and Mail* before he was posted to Beijing as the paper's Asia correspondent. He wrote some very controversial copy not just about China, but about the whole area, the most sensational being a piece about prostitution in the Philippines.

He followed up with a book on the subject. Then he seemed to disappear. A year or two later it was reported in the magazine *Saturday Night* that he was running a brothel in Manila.

Although I did not know Johnson, I took the bare bones of this situation and devised a story of an investigative journalist who travels to the Far East with his young stepson, where he finds his former mentor living with a child prostitute in Bangkok.

I developed the story with Greg's help, thinking he would produce it. However it was decided by someone higher up that the show would be produced in Vancouver by John Juliani. I decided to fly to Vancouver at my own expense to be present at the taping.

John greeted me warmly and invited me to dinner, where I discovered that his own wife was Asian, which may well have accounted for his interest in the story. He had decided to cast their eighteen-year-old son as the protagonist. I thought the taping went well, but when I returned to Toronto, Greg was fairly dismissive and there was some controversy as to whether the piece which was now re-titled *Bangkok Blue* was too risqué for *Morningside*. It was eventually broadcast in the summer months, when traditionally the audiences were smaller. I never learned what response it received from the public, but it was to be my last show for the program, which in any case changed radically when Gzowski left.

Damiano, as head of radio drama and features, was keen to broadcast work of high literary quality. He approached several prominent authors to write scripts for him, but he was not able to offer substantial fees and in any case radio was regarded as small potatoes. James Roy was asked to approach Alice Munro, whom he knew through her work as a volunteer for the Blyth Festival, which, as a local resident, she supported. She gave her consent to an adaptation of *Lives of Girls and Women* and James approached me to do the adaptation. I knew the book well and had the highest respect for all Munro's work, even though she was not as yet famous and an acknowledged master. She stipulated that I work with a woman at CBC that she knew as an editor. Our relationship was not an easy one but I managed to come up with a script that both she and James were satisfied with.

We had a very good cast, with Sheila McCarthy and Kristina Nicoll as the young girls, Del and Naomi. Although they were probably ten to fifteen years older than the characters they were playing, they nailed the adventurous and mischievous nature of Munro's characters. One of the nice things about working in radio is that you don't have to be concerned with the visual appearance of the performers. Another advantage is that the performers have a respect for the words, as that's all there is. Our adaptation was well received, though I never learned what Alice Munro thought of it.

At Damiano's suggestion, I wrote a stage adaptation. The material is so rich in idiom and the detail is so accurate that I thoroughly enjoyed working on it. Munro's characters in her early work inhabit a space that is very close to the world my mother grew up in, and therefore it is very real for me. I showed my adaptation to Jeannette Lambermont, a female director who was working at Stratford, and she reported that they were interested in it, both because it represented Canadian content and because it could be sold as a family show. I sent the script to Alice Munro, who at the time was spending her summers on the West Coast, and in due course received a letter from her agent in New York refusing permission for the adaptation to be performed. She was not prepared to discuss the reasons. Someone suggested it was because I was not a woman. I have no way of knowing whether Alice Munro was influenced by such a rigidly feminist agenda.

I found adaptation an enjoyable exercise. It forced me to expand and stretch my imagination by trying to get inside the head of another writer and also gave me the discipline of adhering to a storyline that someone else had worked out. When Damiano approached me to do another adaptation, I was eager to comply. The work in question was Michel Tremblay's gay novel *The Heart Laid Bare*. I was somewhat amused to find that because of the success of "La Bolduc" I was considered something of an authority on Quebecois literature. My friend Richard Monette told me Tremblay would never agree to let me adapt his work, but in fact he did. Whether he remembered our encounter when I interviewed him in Montreal some few years back or whether he was influenced by the fact that Richard, who had enjoyed such a success with *Hosanna*, was to play the lead, I don't know.

Damiano engaged John Roby to write a musical score, which made a huge contribution to the show. I felt confident enough to make some dialogue additions of my own. Damiano initially questioned this but paid me the compliment of saying he thought the script was seamless. Richard was very well cast as the older man who takes a young lover; as a middle-aged homosexual, he was working in very familiar territory. David Storch found the right combination of youthful arrogance and emotional uncertainty as the young man. The show was considered rather daring in the late '80s and received a positive response from various gay members of the audience, who congratulated Damiano on having the courage to tell their story.

I would do one more hour-length drama for Damiano. My friend Laurier LaPierre had written a biography of his namesake, Sir Wilfred Laurier, and approached Damiano about doing a dramatic adaptation. Damiano asked me if I thought I could work with Laurier and I responded that we were long-time friends. I went up to Ottawa, where Laurier was then living, and we plotted a scenario based on Laurier's life and outlined various essential scenes.

Once we had agreed on the overall shape of the story, Laurier said to me, "I don't know how to do this."

"But I do," I responded. "Why don't I take it away and send you a draft?" Laurier was on the whole pleased with my work but suggested a few changes, including an opening sequence that was more dramatically effective than what I had come up with and got the story off to a more exciting start. Once again we cast mainly French-Canadian actors: Monette as Laurier, Diana Leblanc as his wife, Louise Pitre as his mistress, and Donald Carrier as his rival and possible son. The show was again well-received, and there was some talk of me writing more dramas based on other Canadian historical figures but nothing came of it.

After she left *Ideas*, Geraldine Sherman was given a half-hour Sunday-afternoon show called *State of the Arts*, which contained reviews, snippets of performance, and mini-profiles of artists, writers, and performers. I submitted a proposal to her titled *Bad Boys to the Rescue*. After a shaky first season as artistic director of the Stratford Festival, John Neville decided to invite back two directors who had misbehaved in the past: Brian Macdonald and Robin Phillips. I went up to Stratford with my portable tape recorder and managed to record interviews with both men, as well as short cuts of them in rehearsal. Michael Crabb helped me cut and edit the piece on Macdonald, which was duly aired. I was informed that Geraldine herself would work with me on the Phillips segment.

She greeted me by saying, "I have to admit that your Macdonald piece was better than I expected." I would learn that this sort of comment was usual with Geraldine. A tall woman with rather wild grey hair and long, spiky false nails attached to every finger, she came across as bit of a witch, a role I think she relished. She was quick-witted and had a sharp sense of humour and certainly didn't hold back criticism. "You sound as though you're eating marshmallows," she would say as I recorded my intro, or, "Can't you speak like a normal person?" Such input did nothing to build confidence on my part. But in spite of this we got on not badly. We fought over every piece we worked on together, but at least what we managed to hammer out was what went on the air, whereas working with one of the other producers, I would be told, "I love what you've done," but by the time I heard it, it was more or less unrecognizable.

Geraldine must have received some favourable comment on these initial pieces because she asked me for other ideas. Next I promoted the idea of a piece on my old friend Richard Williams. She was less than enthusiastic, having never heard of him, but when *Who Framed Roger Rabbit* opened in Toronto to rave reviews, and she learned Dick was a Toronto boy, she agreed to let me do it. I was delighted when I got a phone call from Dick's mother, whom I had mentioned. She pretended embarrassment but I could tell she was delighted.

Some weeks later I suggested a piece about Walt Wingfield, the city boy who moves to a farm and has a series of humorous encounters with local characters. I had first seen this one-man show with all the parts acted by Rod Beattie in Orangeville, where it played to a crowd of rural types. They were delighted with it but said, "You couldn't do this in the city; they wouldn't get it." A month or so later it was presented at the Arts and Letters Club in Toronto, where the urban audience was similarly amused but said, "Of course you couldn't do it in the country; people would be offended." Both Dan Needles, the writer, and Rod were former students of mine and we had stayed in touch. Geraldine was less than enthusiastic about the idea of profiling it on her program. "*Farmers*," she said, making a face. "Our show is supposed to be about *Art*." I gave her a tape and she claimed she had lost it.

I followed up with a video, which she said she didn't have time to watch. I kept after her and finally she said, "Okay, go ahead and do your little hayseed drama."

The day after the Wingfield segment aired, the phone at CBC Radio rang off the wall. The head of programming, a rather snotty Englishman who normally didn't have the time of day for me, phoned me at home. "Dear Martin, how can I get in touch with Rod Beattie?" Apparently Peter Gzowski had heard the segment and wanted to air something similar on *Morningside*. Gzowski had both Dan and Rod as guests on his show more than once and this helped them build an audience. They would eventually write and perform half a dozen sequels, and the shows toured across Canada and the northern United States, usually playing to packed houses.

Although Geraldine didn't compliment me on finding the show for her, she was more receptive to my future proposals. The next summer I spent a month in England and returned with interviews I had recorded with Alan Ayckbourn, whom I visited in Scarborough; Peter Brook, who was touring his seven-hour production of *The Mahabharata*; and Lindsay Kemp, whom I caught doing a circus-themed extravaganza at Sadler's Wells shortly before he decamped to Rome. All three interviews went to air and I was able to claim my expenses in England against my broadcast fees.

The next autumn, Geraldine went to Japan for several months with her husband. While she was away, her staff, fed up with her autocratic ways, went to management and persuaded them to take the program away from her. She was succeeded by Anne Gibson, whom I already knew through common friends, who assured me she would be giving me some assignments. However, this didn't happen. Anne was strongly influenced by Urjo Kareda, who I had come to realize was no friend of mine.

One day I was taken to lunch by Damiano. Over coffee he said, "You've had a pretty good inning writing for radio. However, you're an old white male. I'm afraid that's just what we don't want. Don't expect to get any more commissions from the CBC." Damiano and I would remain friends, and a few years later we would be involved in another project together. Eventually he was asked to step down from his position as head of radio drama. At the time, someone said to me, "I guess he just wasn't ethnic enough." My belief is that he was too intellectual for the new management bent on dumbing down the content on our national airwaves.

DOWN MEXICO WAY

I have long believed that successful parenting is demonstrated when a child leaves home and embarks on a life of his or her own. My daughter, Sarah, went to India at the age of seventeen, where she attended an international school before going to Sarah Lawrence College in the United States. My son Guy, after he graduated from high school, worked on a fishing boat on the West Coast to make enough money to travel in Europe. I told him he should do something more interesting than hang around with other expats in London and Paris. He apparently listened to me because he went to Morocco and hitchhiked across the Sahara before coming back to Trent University. He dropped out in his third year so that he could go and work with the contras in Nicaragua. He came back, took his degree, and then went off to Saskatchewan to work with the NDP.

My other son, Ben, dropped out of Jarvis Collegiate and hung around at home until I told him, "You're not going to loaf here all day blowing dope and making wisecracks with your friends. You can damn well get out and get a job." He drove taxis and worked as a night watchman before he took off for Japan, where he taught English as a second language for two years before boarding the Trans-Siberian Railway. He ended up in Minneapolis, where he kicked his drug habit with the help of a quasi-Buddhist offshoot called Eckankar.

Perhaps the fact that we had travelled with our children in Europe, Africa, and the Caribbean influenced them to travel on their own. In any case, none of them returned to live in the family home on a permanent basis. They had been encouraged to receive a good education and take an interest in the arts, but they did not have a conventional grounding in religion. We did sometimes take them to the local Presbyterian church until Ben decided he wanted to attend Sunday school in his Batman costume. I said I was sure Jesus would not be offended, but somehow this incident more or less signalled the end of our affiliation with organized religion. As adults, two of our three children would seek involvement with the life of the spirit: Sarah with the ideas of Joseph Campbell, who was one of her professors, and later with the teachings of Gurdjieff and Jung; Ben with Eckankar and reincarnation. Guy contented himself with occasional consultation with the Tarot. It is interesting to speculate on what habits kids pick up from their parents and what they reject. None of my kids smoke or drink, although I am arguably an alcoholic and smoked heavily until I was almost forty.

Ben was accepted as a mature student and completed his first year of university in Minnesota, then finished his degree at McGill. In Montreal, he lived with his girlfriend of the time, Paule. Both my sons have had girlfriends since they were fourteen and I expected they would marry and settle down. Not so. They each pursued relationships that lasted anywhere from a few months to several years. Guy went into therapy briefly to discuss his issues with commitment. It apparently resolved nothing. Ben broke with Paule and returned to the United States. In due course, we received word that he was about to be married to a fellow Eck adherent named Sharon. We all boarded a plane for Minneapolis to attend the wedding.

We were not sure what to expect: midnight revels in which the Eckists danced naked around a bonfire? Chanting monks in saffron robes? Druidical priestesses trailing mistletoe and ivy in their flowing locks? It turned out the ceremony, though performed in a grove of evergreens, was fairly conventional. Although the clergyperson was a woman in a white, cassock-like outfit, the words she uttered were a fairly conventional mélange of spiritual clichés. The bride was a pretty, dark-haired girl in a conventional wedding dress. Ben had collected some of his buddies as groomsmen who wore suits and white shirts. They had opted to buy Liberty printed bowties but had no idea how to tie them. I was summoned to their dressing room to perform this function, which I had learned from my father before my first formal dance in high school.

There was a reception after the ceremony with tasty food but no alcohol. Guy had quickly picked up that one of the attractions of Eckankar to many of its members was that it functioned as a rehab centre. There were some elders who ran the show, but most of the people at the wedding were kids in their twenties in the process of sorting themselves out. It was evident that these young people came from reasonably affluent, middle-class families and could afford to contribute generously to the organization, not only financially but in terms of time given in attending and leading conferences and seminars. At the end of the afternoon, Ben and Sharon climbed into his robin-egg-blue Camaro and drove off into the sunset, supposedly to live together happily ever after. This is not the way it turned out, but that's another story.

Sarah returned to Toronto, but Judy, Guy, and I had decided to give ourselves a brief holiday. We flew to Mexico City, where we enjoyed the Art Deco splendours of the Hotel Majestic overlooking the Zócalo. The army paraded there at sunrise and sundown when the flag was raised and lowered. We visited the wonderful National Museum to view the impressive remains of Aztec and Mayan sculpture. We viewed the powerful political frescoes of Diego Rivera and the painful paintings of Frida Kahlo and wondered what drew these two completely different artists together.

After a week, we took a bus to the ancient silver-mining town of San Miguel de Allende, which was just beginning to blossom as a winter haven for gringos of an artistic bent. The house we rented belonged to a member of the Rockefeller family. It was built around a pretty patio, which had a tiny wading pool, a fountain, and some shade trees and flowers that were tended by a part-time gardener. There was also a cook, an ample Mexican woman who was accompanied by her pretty but rather surly daughter. The daughter went shopping in the market with Guy, who was fluent in Spanish, and learned that her disposition stemmed largely from the fact that as the youngest of the family, she was expected to stay at home and look after her parents until they died.

The cook ruled the kitchen and was unwilling to let any of us prepare food, but we ate out several times a week so that she did not have to prepare dinner seven nights a week. There were a number of good restaurants, not all of which offered only Mexican food. About the third night we were in town, we were eating in one of these bodegas when Judy said, "I'm pretty sure that guy two tables over is Toller Cranston." Toller was a cousin of Judy's on her mother's side and his family had a cottage down the beach. Judy remembered that his parents habitually rented their cottage every summer in order to finance Toller's skating lessons. Although he never won Olympic gold, he single-handedly revolutionized men's figure skating. Now semi-retired, he lived most of the year in San Miguel, though still flying all over the world to judge competitions.

Guy and I went over to Toller's table and he greeted us cordially. It was immediately obvious that he was particularly taken with Guy, whom he asked to join his table. He invited Guy to go swimming with him the next day at a spring in a nearby town. He also invited all of us to his birthday party (he wouldn't disclose the number) in about a week's time at his substantial estate in town.

After dinner Guy and I went to a small bar to hear some local musicians sing and play. We noticed two middle-aged women sitting with a rather aggressive Mexican man at a nearby table. They signalled us to join them. It soon became clear the man was trying to hit on them and they were looking to us to help them fend off his advances. The Mexican eventually took off and we stayed and chatted with the women. They were pleasant but not at all glamorous, probably two grandmothers on holiday. I asked them about themselves and they told us they were professional gamblers. They played blackjack and poker for the house at a casino in a nearby town.

During the day, Guy and I explored San Miguel, which had been prosperous in the preceding centuries because of a nearby silver mine. The centre of town was a tree-shaded square surrounded by a few rather grand seventeenth-century palaces and a small but elaborately decorated cathedral. There were frequent religious parades and pageants and the square often featured *mariachis*, local musicians with colourful jackets and huge sombreros. The townspeople and the tourists would gather in the square at sundown to hear them, exchange gossip, and buy sweets from street vendors, while hundreds of blackbirds came home to roost in the trees that surrounded the square. It might all have been arranged by a tourist agency, but as far as I could make out it was completely authentic.

On another evening we were having dinner when we were hailed by Don Owen. Don had been a filmmaker in Canada in the '60s, and his early works starring Jackie Burroughs, though now more or less forgotten, had been some of the most original and colourful movies of the time, paving the way for various actors who starred in some early CBC dramas. Don was no longer active as a filmmaker and was staying in San Miguel at the house of his friend Annette Cohen. Annette invited us to a dinner party, a diverse gathering that included the painter Gary Slipper, an octogenarian actress whose daughter had been with us at Trinity, and a jolly woman from Nova Scotia named Bonnie. Like Don, Bonnie was a Buddhist; she was also a belly dancer.

A few days later Bonnie invited us to a party at her house. The party was intended to show off the skills of a few of her belly-dancing pupils, who performed for our edification. At the end of this exhibition, Bonnie took to the floor. Although at least fifty years old and somewhat overweight she was easily the most accomplished practitioner of her art. She even persuaded me to get up on the floor and perform with her, which elicited applause from the assembly, not because of my skill, but rather because of my audacity, although I did hear one of the Mexicans sitting around the floor call out, *"Más suave, más suave."*

Toller's party was very grand. We had all been told to dress in white and silver. He greeted us at the gate and made comments on our outfits, some of which were quite elaborate, others less so. We were seated according to his assessment of our sartorial efforts. Toller himself wore a white Mexican wedding shirt that was open to the waist and about twenty-five pounds of silver jewellery. Mariachis had been hired and we were invited to dance. We were also invited, indeed entreated, to buy at least one of his paintings, which were arrayed around the grounds. We mingled with the guests over drinks. We already knew Julia and Robert Foster from Toronto. Julia was the chairman of the board of the Stratford Festival and was presumably a guest because Toller was promoting the idea of a show in which he would play a leading role.

We also knew Toller's mother, Stuart, an opinionated and sharp-tongued woman who had deliberately shunned his dress code for a frock of navy blue with pink polka dots. Following drinks, we were all seated according to Toller's directions. He sat at a table with his mother, his former skating coach, and a large German woman who managed his estate. Even though we were at another table we could appreciate that Toller was deliberately fanning the competitive instincts of these three women. Partway through dinner we began to hear piteous cries from one of the small *casitas* on the estate, which Toller rented to paying guests. Toller commanded that we ignore this distraction, but his German manageress decided to investigate. She came back to report their guest was having a heart attack and she wanted to call an ambulance. Stuart demanded that she be given the phone and called the medics. She then denounced Toller as a selfish and unfeeling narcissist in front of the entire company and announced that she was leaving and would fly home on the next available plane. Toller yelled after her that she had deliberately ruined his party and he never wanted to see her again.

After our stay in San Miguel, Judy returned to Toronto, but Guy and I went on to Oaxaca, a southern city also favoured by North Americans. I had been invited to visit my old friend Jackie Burroughs, who had taken some of her earnings from the highly successful television series *Road to Avonlea* and built herself a house on the outskirts of this old Mayan town. I had known Jackie as a young actress with a fresh and pretty face and a curvaceous figure. She was now thin as a rail and looked about eighty, although she could not have been more than fifty-five. She drove into town to pick us up and take us to her hacienda.

The house was small but decorated in a highly individual style which combined Mexican artifacts with a variety of other elements that had caught her fancy: Javanese batiks, bits of African sculpture, and some pieces of English china which she had inherited from her mother, an extremely tough-minded British woman with whom Jackie warred incessantly until the old woman died. We sat in her garden, which she had created completely from scratch. "I came to gardening late, but I've discovered it's a great way to get rid of my fascistic tendencies. I look at some plant that's got beyond itself and say, 'Off with its head,' like the Queen of Hearts in *Alice*."

She offered to make us margaritas but explained that she no longer drank alcohol herself. When her daughter came to live with her in Los Angeles some years ago, she realized that the girl had a drug problem. The two of them joined Alcoholics Anonymous and Jackie sent a completely cured Zoe back to live with her father in Kingston. "Of course I still smoke like a chimney, but I have to have some vice to keep me going. I still go to AA meetings when I'm in Canada but not here. All the members talk about is the servant problem and I find that excessively boring. If these snooty American bitches would take the trouble to learn Spanish, they'd get along fine with the people who work for them."

After a delicious lunch, Jackie took us back into town and walked us about showing us the market, the elaborate rococo churches, and a couple of houses with exquisite gardens. We climbed up the pyramid of Monte Albán and drove to a smaller Mayan ruin some thirty kilometres to the south. Jackie told us she had been introduced to Oaxaca by Margaret Atwood and her partner, Graeme Gibson, many years earlier, when few North Americans knew about the town. I told her that we had seen Don Owen in San Miguel and she made a wry face. "Don was a real talent. It's too bad he's become so full of himself. I fucked him once. He wasn't very good." She suddenly turned a cartwheel, revealing that she wasn't wearing any underpants. "I did that in the middle of my audition for Robin Phillips, so of course he hired me. It had nothing to do with talent." I already knew that Jackie's greatest asset was her spontaneity.

We stayed three days with Jackie, who took an instant liking to Guy. The two of them went on a long walk every day. I knew Jackie had a taste for young men. And they shared an outrageous sense of humour. She was delighted when Guy joined in a game of volleyball with some young Mexican boys, and Jackie insisted on joining in the game herself. She had in fact been quite athletic in her youth, when she was head girl at Branksome Hall.

The day before we left Oaxaca, Jackie commented, "Your son is quite the loverboy. I understand both of you want to spend your last days at the seashore. I recommend a fishing village called Puerto Escondido that can be reached by a small plane."

We were the only people on board. The pilot suggested one of us might like to join him in the cockpit. I recommended Guy do so. We flew just above the treetops across a rolling landscape for about twenty minutes and landed in a field. Guy informed me he had flown the plane most of the way, but the pilot wouldn't let him land it. We walked towards the sea and then along the beach. We found a small hotel and booked one of their six rooms. The next two days we spent on the beach. I have always enjoyed walking along beside the incoming waves and watching the people coming and going. Here, they were mainly young people from a variety of countries: tall, tanned young men and some very pretty girls with impressive figures, their round breasts and buttocks barely covered by bikinis. I went for a long swim each day while Guy scuba dived.

On our last evening we ate dinner with a young Australian and his Danish girlfriend. I polished off a brandy and, because we had to catch an early flight the next morning, I decided to head back to our hotel. The Australian had discovered a disco down the beach and Guy was readily persuaded to go for a farewell dance. About four in the morning, I awoke when he returned to our bedroom. "I've met this wonderful girl."

"I don't want to hear about it." I rolled over and went back to sleep. I got up at seven and packed my bag with the few clothes I had brought on this last leg or our holiday. I shook Guy and he opened his eyes.

"I'm staying here."

"Don't be silly."

"I'm serious."

"Is she that wonderful?"

He nodded and closed his eyes. I stood over him for a minute and then shrugged. I knew how stubborn he could be. I got out his plane ticket and put it on the dresser along with what remained of my Mexican money.

About ten days later, Guy reappeared at our house in Toronto. He flopped on the sofa with a mournful sigh.

"What happened to Ms. Wonderful?"

"She was wonderful, but it didn't work out."

For once, I curbed my curiosity.

UP AND DOWN IN LONDON, PARIS, AND TORONTO

When I was almost sixty my father died and left me and my brother handsome legacies, although he left the bulk of his fortune to the charitable foundation he had established some ten years earlier. I had never inherited money before and it kind of went to my head. "Now I'm rich," I thought. "I can do whatever I like." Big mistake. But it provided some fun while it lasted. I could eat at upscale restaurants, drink better wine, stay in grander hotels when I travelled.

For the next few years I made an annual visit to London. I had become accustomed to staying with Powell and Peter at the vicarage. When Peter inherited a substantial house in Sussex, I began staying with Powell's longtime friend and literary collaborator, Rodney Archer, in a house he had bought in Spitalfields in east London. The house was a narrow eighteenth-century townhouse. Rodney and his mother bought it for forty thousand pounds. It had all the original panelling and plasterwork, but no electricity and no plumbing. Gradually, over a period of two decades, they renovated it and in time the location became fashionable. They began to have some well-known neighbours, including the artists Gilbert and George, whose performance pieces included a two-hour show of them eating dinner. Rodney had a good eye, and he slowly filled his house with treasures accumulated from markets and junk shops, including William Morris furniture, Art Deco screens, and paintings by lesser-known British artists of the early twentieth century. The house was not exactly convenient. I slept on the third floor and travelled down to the loo in the basement, but Rodney was agreeable and entertaining and had a wide variety of interesting friends who often popped in unexpectedly: out-of-work film actors, a forgotten Georgian poet, a handsome trooper in the Household Cavalry, and a black masseur who turned out to be the son of an evangelical clergyman. Rodney served them tea in hand-painted china cups in his narrow garden, which featured, improbably, a silver birch tree and eighteenth-century cast-iron urns filled with orange and yellow nasturtiums.

Gradually, Spitalfields became fashionable and Rodney's street attracted celebrities such as Siân Phillips, the ex-wife of Peter O'Toole. Rodney met a decorator at a market who convinced him that he should sell half his treasures on the internet and use the proceeds to redecorate the first two floors, where he could display the remaining half, which included, among other items, Oscar Wilde's fireplace. By now, the house was worth several million pounds and Rodney was able to meet his tax bill by turning his sitting rooms into an art gallery and inviting visitors including, such celebrities as Stephen Fry. In fact, he would become something of a celebrity himself, and he thoroughly enjoyed his newfound acclaim as a connoisseur and eccentric personality.

My friend Robert Troop had an office in Golden Square where he edited a number of magazines. We frequently lunched in the old Café Royal in Regent Street or at The Carvery in a hotel on Piccadilly Circus. I went several evenings a week to dinner at Robert's house in Barnes. His wife, Liz, was a published novelist and scriptwriter for BBC Radio. Sometimes we went to the theatre.

I remember an excellent production of *The Way of the World* in which Judi Dench played Millamant. I had first seen her years earlier as Viola in *Twelfth Night* at Stratford-upon-Avon, and I followed her career with growing enthusiasm. She was hands-down the best Millamant, the best Lady Macbeth, and the best Cleopatra I have ever seen. On another occasion I took all my London friends to see Stephen Sondheim's *Follies*, featuring a bevy of well-known British musical stars. I mused on the way home that I had spent a thousand dollars and my friends, far from being entertained, hated the show one and all.

Robert and Liz and I went to a number of musical concerts at Royal Festival Hall and several smaller venues. None of us were competent musicians, but Robert's older son, Mark, was rapidly developing into an accomplished pianist. He was engaged to an Indian soprano, Patricia Rozario, and we went to some of their concerts. She would go on to have a successful career singing at Glyndebourne and in various European opera houses and become a sort of muse for several English composers. I attended their wedding in Hanover Square, which was attended by members of her family who had flown to London from Goa and included several brothers who were merchant bankers in various European capitals.

The wedding was also attended by Sir Peter Hall, whom I met at the reception afterwards at the Basil Street Hotel. He had taken an interest in one of Robert's novels, *The Hammering*, which he had just optioned with a view to basing a film on it. He was a big, jovial man and promoted the idea that Robert and I should collaborate on a film script for him, perhaps a political thriller. A few days later at lunch, Robert and I roughed out a scenario whose central figure was to be a Canadian cabinet minister who was trying to sell nuclear reactors to a foreign country. We decided to set the action in Rio de Janeiro, partly because Robert's father had been an executive in the Canadian company Brazilian Traction. Both Robert and I had been in Rio at different times, and we felt we could write about it convincingly. The principal conflict would be between the minister and his young son who was working as a priest in the *favelas*, or slums, of the tropical city.

We thoroughly enjoyed mapping out the plot and we then began to work on scenes individually. Before the advent of the internet, we had to mail our work back and forth across the Atlantic. As would happen with other collaborations, it fell to me to stitch the various pieces together. It gradually became apparent that Peter Hall was not really interested in our idea, primarily because he could not raise production money unless he could interest a major star. The names of Christopher Plummer and Donald Sutherland were bandied about, but at that time neither of them was a major film star. Before long it was clear to me that Robert had also lost interest in the project.

Back in Toronto, I submitted the film script to Dick Nielsen, who had just finished shooting Timothy Findley's *The Wars*, directed by Robin Phillips. He expressed an interest in it and suggested I submit it to the CBC, which I did. Dick was interested in anything which had political content, and I thought the script had a chance with him. At the time, he and his partner Pat Ferns had the backing of Torstar, the company that controlled the *Toronto Star*. However, Torstar changed hands, and the new owners reacted strongly against the homosexual content of *The Wars* and withdrew their funding. The picture did get made but received very limited distribution and was not well received critically. Two years later, the CBC phoned me to say they thought our script had some value. Did I have a producer? "Not anymore," I was forced to admit.

I had decided that the script might be adapted for the stage. Robert wrote to say I could do whatever I wanted with the story, so I got to work on a stage version. Because the film script had contained quite a bit of action, including an attempt by one of the characters to blow up the monumental statue of Christ that towers over Rio on the mountain of Corcovado, it was less vivid than the original version. However, I was able to persuade Robin Phillips to read it and he found it interesting. By this time he had left Stratford and was running a repertory company at the Grand Theatre in London, Ontario. He told me that he was thinking of including the play in his second season there. However, his first season ended in financial disaster; the board dismissed him and opted for less expensive and experimental work in the future. Robin and I continued to stay in touch and eventually found another project on which we believed we could collaborate, but that lay several years down the road.

I next approached Sean Gillespie, a stage manager with ambitions to direct. He started to put a cast together led by Michael Hogan, who read the script and agreed to play the lead, possibly with his wife, Susan, playing opposite him. We read some actors, including a young Stephen Ouimette, and the prospects seemed promising. Then Michael's agent, Perry Zimmer, called to tell me Michael was not available. (I would later learn that Michael was unaware Perry had turned down our offer, a technique not unusual with high-profile agents, who prefer to keep their clients available to make more profitable movie and TV deals.) A week later, Sean discovered he had AIDS. The project seemed doomed, and I abandoned it, at least for the time being.

In the meantime I had formed a friendship with the actor Richard Monette, with whom I had worked a good many times in radio. I thought the play might provide a vehicle for him as an actor. He read and liked it, but at the time he had more or less given up on acting, having had several attacks of severe stage fright. He had just begun to direct in smaller theatres in Toronto. John Neville offered him a chance to direct a main-stage production at Stratford. His *Taming of the Shrew* starring Colm Feore and Goldie Semple established him as an important director. Set in the 1950s and somewhat based on his own dysfunctional family, it was funny and warm and a big hit with audiences. It set the tone for what would become his strongest work, comedy with heart.

I had first seen Richard as a teenage actor in a university drama festival at Hart House Theatre. It was immediately apparent to me that he had extraordinary stage presence and I went to see his work whenever I had the chance: his teenage Hamlet at the Crest; his leading role in *The Little Drummer Boy* when the Crest was followed up by a repertory company at The Royal Alex; and the play that put him on the map, *Hosanna* at Bill Glassco's Tarragon Theatre. Richard became a frequent visitor at our house on Sherbourne Street. We shared a love of good food and drink, conversation about theatre and music, and sharp-edged gossip.

We decided to take a holiday together in the winter months between the Stratford seasons. Judy was teaching but I was free to travel. Richard opted for France as our destination. I had some knowledge of the country, particularly Paris, and I lined up a couple of writing gigs for one or two of my magazines. I found a small hotel on the Rive Gauche, where we made our way after landing at Charles de Gaulle Airport. Across the street was a fire station. Richard was happy to watch the young *pompiers* horsing around in the street. I was certainly not bilingual but my French was serviceable. "I haven't spoken French since I was fifteen. You will have to deal with the language," announced Richard. After two days he said to me, "Your French is very game, Martin, but I think I can do as well." And he began to speak his mother tongue again after a hiatus of over twenty years.

We walked all over Paris, along the quays and across the bridges. It was on one of these that Richard stopped and told me that he had spent a weekend in Paris when he was a young actor working in London with his then-girlfriend Francine. She suddenly turned to him, took from her finger the ring Richard had given her and said, "Richard, you have promised me the world, but you haven't given it to me." She dropped the ring in the Seine and walked away out of his life. Obviously, she had a thing for actors as she later married Donald Sutherland, but Richard was so discouraged he returned immediately to London.

The next day we bought a baguette, some cheese, and a bottle of Nuits-Saint-Georges and had an alfresco lunch in the Tuileries gardens, where for three centuries homosexuals have cruised each other. Afterwards we wandered through the tree-lined streets of the Marais. The Canadian painter Joe Plaskett lived there in a sixteenth-century house full of treasures he had accumulated over a thirty-year residence. We visited him for tea. He was tended by a handsome young Romanian lad, an aspiring artist, who made a date with Richard. It became apparent that Joe was quite deaf, so whether he heard about this assignation was not clear. He told us about some of the more obscure museums, such as the Cluny and the Guimet, both of which we visited in addition to the Louvre and the d'Orsay. It being late winter, they were not overly crowded.

We were asked by my friend Martin Stone to a reception at the residence of the Canadian Embassy, which turned out to be the *hôtel particulier* that had once been owned by the duc de la Rochefoucauld. We felt distinctly underdressed, as we had not thought to bring suits. At the reception we encountered Adrienne Clarkson, who was serving in Paris as the agent for the Government of Ontario. She arranged for us to have lunch with Carlos Ott, the Uruguayan-Canadian architect who was designing the new opera house at the Place de la Bastille. He was a charming fellow. He gave us hard hats and walked us around the site. Adrienne also suggested we go to a small gallery for the *vernissage* of a show by a Canadian artist named Dako who worked in a cartoon style based on old comic books full of balloons: WHAM, SLURP, KAPOW. We found the gallery, with difficulty, down a rather muddy alley. It was a old garage filled with young artists: women with green and blue hair sporting ripped black stockings and low-cut bustiers, men in skin-tight jeans or kilts overlaid with clanging metal chains. When I got back home, I wrote a piece for *Toronto Life* about these two Canadian artists, which I titled Ott Dako (Art Deco, get it?). I thought this was rather witty but my editor nixed it.

Richard was of course keen to see as much theatre as possible. We went to the old opera house, the Palais Garnier, and sat in a box, or *baignoire*, to watch a production of Handel's *Julius Caesar in Egypt*. The design was a mixture of classical, Napoleonic, and modern styles. Caesar wore an early-nineteenth-century uniform and kept one hand stuck in his waistcoat. Cleopatra was dressed rather like Theda Bara and vamped her way around the stage. When she sang an aria about how Egypt would rise again, oil rigs appeared on the cyclorama. In the opening scene Caesar appeared upstage and looked down on an assembly of miniature pyramids, obelisks, and sphinxes. In the last scene when he was about to depart, some of his soldiers packed these treasures into crates marked "SPQR" and hauled them away.

Richard enjoyed this spectacle but he was much more enamoured of a production of two early Molière farces at the Comédie-Française. The actors were dressed in seventeenth-century costumes, and the productions featured some very deft comic business, including a very lifelike little dog whom one of the actors manipulated with great skill and which pissed in his face on cue. Richard was fascinated to see the old chair that Molière sat in when he played *Le Malade Imaginaire* and in which he is rumoured to have died in the middle of a performance. Richard managed to sit in it for a minute after the show before an usher threw us out of the theatre.

We also saw a brilliant Feydeau farce at the Théâtre des Champs-Élysées, in which the actors did some comic business that had all the precision and invention of the Marx Brothers; a pageant-like musical based on the life of Jesus in which the actor playing Christ literally whipped the hawkers vending chocolate bars and cold drinks; a show in an old circus arena featuring horses ridden by singing gypsies; and we travelled to the outskirts of Paris and sat for three-quarters of an hour in a light rain while waiting for Mnouchkine's three-hour *Oresteia*, played without a break in the style of the Kathakali dancers from southern India.

Mnouchkine was at this time at the height of her fame as the most imaginative theatre director in Europe, but both Richard and I thought this production boring and ridiculous.

We sampled the famous restaurants of Paris: we had an opulent lunch at Maxim's and savoured the fading glories of the Belle Époque; we had a delicious rabbit fricassee at Le Vert Galant at the tip of the Île de la Cité, which was supposedly a favourite haunt of Henri IV; we consumed oysters and drank Chablis at the Brasserie Lipp, surrounded by people who we took to be the reigning literati of the day; we ate roast duck and drank champagne at La Closerie des Lilas, where Fitzgerald and Hemingway sparred in the '20s; and we met Mavis Gallant at the old haunt of Sartre and de Beauvoir, Les Deux Magots. Mavis was deliciously acerbic and delighted us with tales of Herbert Whittaker as a mama's boy when they both worked for the *Gazette* in Montreal in the '40s.

Before we left Toronto, Joan Chalmers had taken me aside at a reception and said in her husky contralto, "I want you to promise me you will see that Richard gets laid in Paris." On our last evening, I took him to the Opera Baths on the rue Louis-le-Grand.

It was then the most elaborate bathhouse I had ever attended and featured not only lounges, private cabins, and dark rooms, but a large swimming pool surrounded by little tables where handsome, scantily clad waiters served excellent food and drink. Richard took up with an Arab lad while I sat and drank a half bottle of Sancerre and watched a gaggle of good-looking lads cavorting naked in the pool. We had planned to visit Versailles and the Châteaux of the Loire, but we enjoyed Paris so much that we decided to forgo these delights and save them for another time.

On the plane home, after a few Scotches, I pressed Richard into talking about *Power Play*, my play set in Rio. He would be willing to direct it if I could raise the necessary funds. I had already approached Urjo Kareda, suggesting a co-production with Tarragon, but he flatly refused to consider the idea. I then approached Mallory Gilbert, the manager of the Tarragon. She offered to rent me the main space at a quite reasonable rate for three weeks starting in mid-September, before their season began. The timing was good for Richard and we set about casting the show.

As Richard had already been tapped as the next artistic director for the Stratford Festival, he had no trouble persuading actors to work for him. Albert Millaire agreed to play the cabinet minister, with Peter Boretski as a sort of cynical fixer and Goldie Semple as the lady journalist who tries to uncover the underlying machinations of this pair of schemers. For the role of the son, a priest inspired by Che Guevara, Richard chose a young actor just out of theatre school, Frank Zotter, and as his sidekick, a Brazilian street kid, Fabrizio Filippo, who had already made a name for himself working for Buddies in Bad Times. It was a highly talented cast; they seemed to like the script and set to work with a will under Richard's direction. Richard was witty and inventive. He was fun to work with and the cast had a thoroughly good time. My old friend and collaborator Martha Mann devised a clever set and some colourful costumes, and my daughter Sarah painted somewhat surrealistic backdrops.

Richard dived into rehearsal without much preparation. It wasn't long before I realized the script needed a dramaturgical going-over by an experienced play doctor. Unfortunately I didn't see this until we were well into rehearsal. The early part of the play was satirical, with the cabinet minister bluffing his way through the deal and his son playing a double role: a do-gooding priest by day, a revolutionary commando by night. Richard did say to me that there was a problem of tone when the son was killed near the end of the play. This undercut the humour, but by this time a major rewrite was not feasible. Richard's solution was to say to me, "More jokes, Martin, more jokes."

A further complication was the fact that five of the actors in the cast were gay. Peter Boretski, to his credit, did not allow himself to become involved with any of the younger actors. But it was clear almost from the outset that Richard had a crush on Frank. The young actor was just on the point of coming out and was not anxious to tie himself to an older man. Richard wooed him ardently, saying, "If you're not ready, I'll wait for you." Their relationship was not improved when Frank was discovered in his dressing room *in flagrante* with one of the other young actors. The shenanigans carried on between the younger actors did not seriously affect the performance of the play, but it did make for a rather bumpy emotional atmosphere.

The play was greeted with applause by the opening night audience, which included many of my friends, who rallied round in support of me and my work. My long-time friend John Uren, a former publicist of the Stratford Festival, took charge of marketing the show, and there were some favourable articles in the press in advance of the show, particularly as Richard's directorial star was obviously on the rise. But the reviews were universally bad. Not just bad, totally negative. Only Robert Cushman in the *Post* had a good word to say for the production, but he made it clear he thought the script was execrable. We played to middling houses for two weeks and cancelled the last week. Several people told me they enjoyed the show, but although the cast continued to give it their best shot, I realized it was a flop. It had cost me almost a hundred thousand dollars to produce and the box office was perhaps ten thousand. As I had just received a generous inheritance, I could afford the loss, but it was still shaming.

As was my custom, I threw a closing night party for the cast.

It was a jolly affair. The actors seemed not to have been badly wounded by the notices and they were in a mood to party. The young kids lolled on the deck behind the house and blew dope. The older contingent sat in the living room and drank whisky or gin. My friend Bill Glassco had joined the party and when my wife came down the stairs, he and I rose to our feet. The rest of the company were amazed. "I thought that only happened in Victorian plays," said Goldie. The party was a nice finish to what had been for me a decidedly mixed experience. It did not seem to have fundamentally affected my relationship with Richard. But in assessing the situation, I felt strongly I shouldn't be trying to write plays. However, the habit of forty years is not so easily abandoned.

THE STRATFORD EXPERIENCE

It became apparent in the late 1980s that Richard Monette was a prime candidate to become artistic director of the Stratford Festival. Because we had become good friends, we discussed this possibility. Richard was uncertain that he wanted to take on this responsibility, which he rightly realized would mean that he could no longer devote as much of himself to the pleasures of the flesh. I encouraged him to see that running the Festival was what his whole life had been leading up to. I remember we spent a whole day with Martha Henry and her then-partner Rod Beattie discussing whether they might accept a joint directorship. Richard came away from this discussion convinced that this would be unworkable. The attempts in the past (and indeed the future) to have the festival run by more than one leader proved unfeasible. I knew that Richard was being interviewed by members of the board. He didn't reveal to me that he had been appointed until the night before the official announcement, but I knew when I attended a party at the festival theatre several months earlier, when Colleen Blake, the assistant general manager, came across the floor to greet me effusively and tell me that the deal had been struck.

It was widely assumed that I would be appointed as Richard's right-hand man. Both Brian Bedford and Christopher Newton questioned me about this. I told Christopher I couldn't imagine why Richard would pay me a salary if he could get my advice for free. Certainly if Richard had offered me a job then at the Festival I would have accepted, but he didn't. Shortly after his appointment, Richard said to me, "The critics hate you and they know we are friends, so I'm not putting us in a position where they can beat up on us." The truth was a little more complicated.

One factor was the failure of our production of *Power Play* at the Tarragon. Shortly after that, Richard was asked by Martha Henry, who was then the artistic director of the Grand Theatre in London, to direct a version of *Whatever Happened to Baby Jane?* as a vehicle for Kate Reid and Janet Wright. Richard fingered me to write the script, which I did. It was rejected by the author's agent in Los Angeles. I later learned that he had an offer for a musical version, which would have made a lot more money, although in fact that production never took place. I would learn that two failures in a row was as much as Richard's tolerance would brook. Richard had become convinced I was a loser.

After the failure of *Power Play*, I embarked on a series of adaptations. I felt that I could learn from working on material of better writers than I, and I believe that in the long run I did. Over the next ten years, I worked on a radio script based on Margaret Atwood's *Cat's Eye*, a stage script based on Alice Munro's *Lives of Girls and Women*, a film script of Michel Tremblay's *The Heart Laid Bare*, a stage version of Robertson Davies' *World of Wonders*, and a musical based on John Glassco's *Memoirs of Montparnasse*. For various reasons, mostly too boring to go into, none of these adaptations was permitted to be performed. But it did give me the advantage of working with some very high-quality material.

Once in office, Richard continued to consult me as an adviser on programming and casting. In the early days of his artistic directorship, he did not have the full confidence of his staff. However, he built a loyal team, whose principal members in his early years were his assistant, Antoni Cimolino, and his publicist, Janice Price. I first met Antoni when Richard was directing *Romeo and Juliet* at the Festival a year before he became artistic director. Richard learned that Antoni had been cast as Romeo and wanted to let him know. Antoni was delivering pizza in the town. Richard and I set out in my car and followed Antoni through the streets of Stratford. He obviously thought he was being pursued by weirdos. He drove furiously back to his house, ran inside, and turned out all the lights. We knocked on the door for some time before he cautiously opened up. He was of course delighted at the news of his casting and we have remained friends ever since.

Antoni was to become a key figure in Richard's reign at Stratford. Not only was he utterly loyal, he was a shrewd and outspoken judge of what plays would sell, what actors should play various roles, how to deal with the board, and where he could get money from both private philanthropists and government officials. I can remember lunching with Antoni when he said, "I'm going into Toronto to get a million dollars." He came back later in the day and reported, "Well, it wasn't exactly a snap, but I got it." And this was back in the days when a million dollars was a substantial piece of cash.

Antoni became a sort of surrogate son to Richard, who was godfather to his children Gabriel and Sofia. Every year at Christmas, Richard would prepare twelve bags of gifts for the two children, to be opened on the twelve days of Christmas. Richard could be extremely generous to his close friends: Otto and Evelyn Beyer, Joseph Shaw, Bennett Solway, me and my wife Judith, Domini Blythe, and his brother Mark, and Mark's two wives, Christine and Judy. He was also generous to his various lovers. "In spite of the fact that I am fun, all my lovers have left me," Richard once said to me. What he didn't say was that, in spite of his generosity, he treated his lovers like shit. Eventually they got tired of the put-downs and public humiliations and found themselves other, more compatible companions. I remember saying to him one occasion, "If we're going to continue to be friends, Richard, you must stop insulting me in public."

Richard's appointment as artistic director at Stratford was greeted with almost universal enthusiasm. Not only was he a Canadian, but a French Canadian. The superiority of Quebecois culture was touted by any number of Anglo critics and tastemakers, from Herbert Whittaker to Bill Glassco, Scott Symons, and Peter Pearson. Jean Gascon, Denise Pelletier, Michel Tremblay, Marie-Claire Blais, Robert Lepage, and Gilles Maheu have all been hailed as much more talented than any Anglo artists, in my opinion often with reason. Richard rode on the clouds of glory they had blazoned. I remember saying to him that he might as well enjoy the adulation he received when he was anointed, because it would not last indefinitely. And of course it didn't.

Some of Richard's early productions were lauded to the skies. His *Taming of the Shrew*, *As You Like It*, and *Camelot* won critical raves. He was justly commended for putting the festival finances back into the black. But then the tide turned. In July of 2000, in an article titled "Sold Out" in *Toronto Life*, Urjo Kareda wrote: "I cannot argue with Richard's success as artistic director. . . . His instincts for programming, though characterized by middlebrow predictability and unadventurous execution, have nevertheless proven profitable. . . . What was once within living memory a visionary artistic enterprise has now been remade as a show palace with leadership that has greater affinities with P.T. Barnum than with Tyrone Guthrie. . . . Richard who began as a passionate, searching artist has now willed himself to serve as a huckster." The critical fraternity picked up the scent. Richard's performance as an artistic director was critically savaged by Kate Taylor in the *Globe* and even Richard Ouzounian in the *Star*, in spite of the fact that Ouzounian hoped to get work at Stratford as a director. Richard became increasingly hostile to critics, as many of us have when subjected to unremitting attacks.

Although at one point I nearly became a critic, I have had a more or less lifelong aversion to the breed. I have more than once avowed that all critics are freaks. I mean physical freaks: Herbert Whittaker with his acne-scarred face and bad breath; Urjo Kareda's blimpish persona; Gina Mallet, whom John Herbert referred to as a "dwarf in a pantsuit." There's some relation between their physical limitations and their critical perspective that seems to make them mean-spirited. They reserve the right to say nasty things about artists but they still want to be accepted by these same artists as friends and fellow artists.

However much he was abused by critics, Richard was a great favourite with the Stratford board of governors, many of whom became friends of ours, particularly Julia and Robert Foster, Rafe and Jane Bernstein, Sandra and Jim Pitblado, Ellsworth and Janet Levine, and Joan Chalmers. We met these people at receptions and occasionally had dinner with them at the Belfry restaurant but were not close friends. I was reminded of the distinction my former partner Alex Smith made between business friends and personal friends. Most of these people were social friends, pleasant to talk to at parties, but not people to rely on in times of trouble.

Richard was also very popular with the actors in his company, particularly the inner circle who played leading roles in his productions. His rehearsals were fun: he tossed off smart remarks, did clever, spontaneous imitations, and could act rings around most of his players. In the evenings he held court at a bar called Down the Street that was owned by some of the theatre technicians. He sat in the front window surrounded by his cronies (particularly his musical director, Bert Carriere), rarely left before closing time, and, when he did, was highly unlikely to be sober. But he went home alone. People thought he could have his pick of any of the men in the company but nobody wanted to be known as the artistic director's bum boy. Richard would lament that he could have taught some aspiring young director everything he knew about the theatre, but although he had several eager young assistants, none of them stayed in the theatre long enough to carry on his legacy.

Richard and I took frequent holidays together. We visited Saint Kitts, Saint Martin, Los Cabos, and Provincetown, usually in January. We took a stack of plays, which we read and evaluated. We then discussed casting for the upcoming season. Casting was one of my skills, if I do say so myself. (In fact I worked for Anne Tait for several months after her partner, Diane Polley, died.

Anne asked me to stay on as her business partner but I declined. There were other things I wanted to do that seemed to me more important. Arguably, I was mistaken.) I do think I was some help to Richard in his early years at Stratford, although he did not always take my advice. And of course he didn't have to. That was the essence of our relationship.

Our most ambitious holiday was the second half of a sabbatical that the Stratford board granted him. He spent two months in Italy as the guest of Rafe and Jane Bernstein and visited Rome, Milan, Naples, and Venice. Travelling with the Bernsteins he stayed in grand hotels — the Excelsior in Rome, the Gritti Palace in Venice — and ate at the most fashionable restaurants. He then flew to Athens, where he met me. Athens did not offer quite such grand hostelries but we were greeted by my old friend Ian Vorres, who gave a lavish reception for us at his house in Paionia, which he had converted into an art gallery displaying his collection of modern Greek paintings. The guests included the American ambassador and Ian's long-time friend Henry Wrong, who was just on the point of stepping down from his position as CEO of the Barbican Centre in London. Ian was interested in arranging an exhibition of the gems of his collection there, but Henry looked on the work with a disparaging eye. "I see a faux Picasso, a derivative Matisse, but I'm afraid I don't see anything of startling originality. Would you agree?" Sadly, I thought his evaluation was accurate.

Richard and I spent a week in Athens. We visited the Parthenon, no longer accessible to the casual tourist; the temple of Poseidon at Sounion, crowded at sunset, which was considered the time when viewing was at its best against an Aegean sunset; and the National Museum, which closed early because of a strike. We also saw a splendid production of Molière's *Don Juan* at the National Theatre. It was in demotic Greek, but as we both knew the text, it didn't matter, although we were somewhat discommoded when a young woman in the front row answered a call on her cellphone and talked for fifteen minutes. I hired a car and we drove to Epidaurus. Richard stood at centre stage and recited a speech from *Henry V*. There was applause from a young man who turned out to be from Sudbury. He was travelling alone and had just been robbed. We took him to lunch and gave him a hundred dollars. We drove on frighteningly narrow and windy roads across the Peloponnese to Olympia, then took a ferry across the Bosphorus to Delphi. Both these sacred sites were almost deserted, and we had a sense of their original sanctity for the first time in our stay in Greece.

Richard wanted to see something of the islands. We boarded a cruise ship along with four hundred other people, a mixture of South Americans, Japanese, and Russians. For five days we mainly ate and drank. We visited Mykonos, Santorini, Crete, and Rhodes. At each stop we would be awakened at six in the morning and herded onto a bus. After sitting in the heat for three-quarters of an hour we would be driven to a site: Knossos or the castle of the Knights Templar. A guide who knew rather less than I did about the history of the place would talk at us for half an hour, after which we would be driven to a shop full of plastic statues and badly painted plates, where we would be stuck among junk which we had no intention of buying, before we were returned to our ship. Compared to our freewheeling visit to Greece thirty years earlier, it was highly dispiriting. I couldn't help but be glad I had seen Greece before it had become so tourist-ified.

Our time in Turkey was much more satisfactory. Sailing up the Bosphorus, we got up early to see the sunrise over the minarets of Hagia Sophia and the Blue Mosque. It was like suddenly finding ourselves entering the Arabian Nights. We stayed in the Green Hotel, a former mini-palace close to these two magnificent monuments and a stone's throw from the old Basilica Cistern, into which we descended to view the huge head of Medusa. We stayed for a week in Istanbul and saw the brilliantly coloured mosaics of ancient Byzantine churches, viewed the impossibly oversized jewels displayed in the ancient Ottoman palace of Topkapi, sailed past the luxurious waterside palaces of former *pashas* now owned by Russian millionaires, and drank Turkish coffee in waterside cafés. And we ate splendid dinners at the small but elegant Four Seasons Hotel just around the corner.

We spent another week touring the Aegean coast with a Turkish guide and driver, visiting mainly ancient Greek sites, amphitheatres, temples, and the ruins of Ephesus with its splendid colonnades and what are believed to be the earliest known public toilets. In Smyrna, we sat at a waterfront café and listened to what we initially thought was some native Turkish music. But on closer hearing I was sure I recognized the voice of Loreena McKennitt. Our guide confirmed my impression, adding, "She is a very big star in Turkey." We visited the supposed site of Troy, where Richard and I climbed up a wooden horse, fancifully based on the structure that the Greeks constructed in order to make their way into "the topless towers of Ilium."

We also visited many shops. At the end of our time in Greece, Richard had mailed home a dozen cartons of artifacts he had purchased there. From Istanbul he mailed home twenty-five cartons. One of the results of our outing was that Richard devised his Greek season at Stratford. His production of *Troilus and Cressida* was a triumph and arguably one of the best productions of his career. It featured, among other things, full frontal nudity. One of his female fans said, "I'm coming again. I don't want to miss a single inch." Another said, "But I didn't think the Greeks were circumcised." Obviously she was a stickler for historical accuracy, like the man who wrote to Richard complaining that Cressida should have been played by a fifteen-year-old boy wearing pumpkin pants under his farthingale.

My friend Damiano Pietropaolo told me that he wanted to initiate a series of programs in the Glenn Gould Studio where actors would read plays, which would then be broadcast across the country. His brainwave was that this could be a collaboration between the CBC and either the Shaw or Stratford Festivals. I mentioned the idea to Richard, who expressed interest. Then, one day when Richard and I were visiting the Shaw Festival to see some shows at the end of their season, I received a call from Janice Price, who asked whether anything could possibly come of this idea. As Richard's publicist, she saw this as something that could broaden the Festival's profile across the country. I said, "All right, I'll make a date with Damiano and drive Richard to Toronto to make sure he gets to the meeting. You'd better be there." Janice did show up for the meeting and it was agreed that the idea had legs, but an infusion of capital was needed, probably eighty thousand dollars, mainly to pay the actors. A week later, Janice called Damiano to say she'd found the money from one of the banks.

The series kicked off with Richard playing Hosanna, which immediately gained attention. Richard asked me to direct it. I asked him what he expected me to do and he replied, "Nothing. Just tell Richard Donat how brilliant he is." Subsequently he suggested that I should become producer for the series, but Damiano said, "Of course he could do the job, but he doesn't need the money. I want to hire a young actress who needs the work."

In the next two years I was asked to direct two more shows as part of the series, both of them plays I had directed on stage. For one of them we used the original cast but the second play, *Yeats in Love*, had to be recast, as the original actors were busy playing something else. Richard asked what actors I wanted and I chose Seana McKenna, because I thought she was a terrific actress, and Rod Beattie, with whom I had worked in the past. I was a bit apprehensive about directing Seana, but at the beginning of the session I gave Rod some notes, which he accepted without question. I could tell that Seana listened to this and thought, "I guess this guy knows what he's doing," and when I gave her some directions she accepted them without demur.

We only had two hours to rehearse these shows in the studio and with this particular show I had to contend with Anne Tait, the writer, and Barbara Worthy, the producer, both of whom stopped the rehearsal with suggested changes several times in the first fifteen minutes. After the sixth interruption, I said, "Look, we've got to get through this script at least once this afternoon. So if I hear anything more from either of you ladies, I'm walking." This tactic worked. Afterwards Seana said to me, "Good for you, Martin." Although we never worked together again, we have remained friends and I do think she is arguably the finest stage actress in the country.

Shortly after this production I was having lunch with Damiano when he said to me, "That Janice Price is a terrific woman." It was plain to me that he wasn't just talking about her smarts as a publicist. I happened to know that her marriage had recently broken up, so I said, "Go for it." He did and it resulted in a liaison that lasted several years. Janice applied for the job of general manager of the Stratford Festival and, when she was passed over, resigned as publicist and before long found herself as publicist and then CEO of the Lincoln Centre in New York. Their relationship, which lasted for about four years, confirmed my opinion that my real talent was for bringing people together, even if the effects didn't last forever.

As the fiftieth anniversary of the Stratford Festival approached I told Richard that he should plan a commemorative book to mark the occasion. "You should write it," he told me. I approached Anna Porter, the wife of my brother Bill's old schoolmate Julian Porter, who seemed enthusiastic. When I didn't hear from her after some six months, I got in touch and she said, "I think you'll find Stratford have made plans to publish a book themselves." I called Richard who said, "I don't know anything about it."

I replied, "Don't bullshit me, Richard. Of course you know about it."

"All right. It's a done deal. We've hired Robert Cushman to write the text. But you should do your own book. We'll sell it in our stores."

I approached Kirk Howard at Dundurn with the idea and he agreed to publish my book. I started to work on it and enlisted the help of my then-friend Ramsay Derry to be the editor. He brought in his friend John Lee to be the designer. The Festival gave me access to their photographic files. John and I worked together using the Festival photographs to put together a book that was, if I may say so, visually stunning. Knowing that Stratford was working on an official history, I realized that we would have to bring our book out first if we were to make significant sales, and in fact we were able to do this. Richard then said to me, "I'm afraid we can't sell your book in our stores in competition with our own book."

I responded, "You promised me you would sell my book in your stores. If you renege on this, I will hire a lawyer and go to the media and make as much trouble for you as I can, and you will not like it." It came out well ahead of their official book and was a damn sight more colourful, partly because Cushman, though a good writer and arguably the most knowledgeable and intelligent critic in Toronto, did not have experience of fifty years of the Festival as I had.

I organized two book launches in Toronto: one at Massey College, attended by the grandees of the Festival including the Pitblados and the Fosters, as well as Bill Hutt, Bill Needles, and Martha Henry; and another at the Drama Centre, attended by Ron Bryden, Brian Parker, and other academic pooh-bahs. The book received favourable reviews, although it had competition from Cushman's book, which appeared subsequently, and a book of Richard Ouzounian's interviews with a number of Stratford actors.

Because there were three books, none of us made any money, although I suspect Cushman and Ouzounian received substantial advances, which I didn't. The cost of setting up the book launches effectively wiped out the money I received from royalties. But my book did sell for a season or two, in spite of the viciously negative review that it received in the *Globe* from the young playwright Jason Sherman, who must have wanted to get back at all theatre critics. I can understand his negative bile. Antoni Cimolino had the good grace to call me and compliment me on the book. He also informed me that in his discussions with Anna Porter, she never mentioned my name. Such is the duplicity of Canadian publishers. My book was for sale in the Stratford theatre stores for a decade and, if nothing else, the photographs were worth the now-discounted price. Of course, because of the deal my publisher made with the Festival I no longer receive royalties.

Given the various snubs and disappointments I have chronicled it may seem strange that I have an abiding affection for the Stratford Festival and consider my relationship with Richard one of the richest of my life. It was rather like a long-term marriage: you give what you have to give and receive whatever is on offer. It did not interfere with my real marriage. Judy knew that my friendship with Richard did not involve sex and she truly enjoyed Richard's company. They exchanged recipes, occasionally went to the theatre or dinner together, and sent each other flowers on birthdays and at Christmas. Richard often stayed at our house when he was in town, which he preferred to a hotel. We laughed and gossiped and ate and drank and entertained mutual friends: Ben Solway and Diana Leblanc and Joseph Shaw. Richard did riotously funny imitations of friends and colleagues, especially me.

When Raymond O'Neill called early one morning to tell me Richard had suffered a massive heart attack and died, I was not surprised. His last years were not pleasant to watch. He was drinking and smoking heavily. After he stepped down as artistic director, he told his agent, Larry Goldhar, that he wanted to work. Larry set him up for a film and he duly came up to Toronto to audition. Afterwards he told me, "I didn't get the role. I wasn't right for it. But if I had been cast, I couldn't have done it. I just don't have the stamina anymore." After his death, a number of people said, "What a waste." I can't agree. In his fourteen-year reign he perfected his last great role: artistic director of the Stratford Festival. He worked hard and he played hard. He achieved his life.

ESCAPADE

Back when I was a teenage actor with the Toronto Children Players, Dorothy Goulding produced a playlet based on an Aboriginal legend called "He Who Makes Music." The play involved a group of young boys aged between ten and twelve who wore masks representing a frog, a coyote, a woodpecker, and a squirrel. Apart from the masks the boys wore nothing but a loincloth. Because they were supposed to be native children they were to wear reddish-brown body makeup, which was purchased from a man who sold theatrical supplies. Mrs. G decided that he was not to be allowed to apply the body paint himself; this task was to be entrusted to Powell Jones and myself, whom she considered responsible. The four boys were assigned to an upstairs dressing room where they stripped to the buff. Powell and I sponged the liquid onto their skinny white bodies and then turned on a fan to quicken the drying process. Of course we did not touch their genitals, but the whole process must have had underlying carnal vibrations that were picked up by at least one of the young players, David Earle.

I was not particularly close to David at that time. I hung out with actors who were closer to my age. He did not pursue a career as an actor but instead trained as a dancer at the National Ballet School and later in New York with Martha Graham and José Limón. Eventually he returned to Toronto with his lover Peter Randazzo, where he lived with his former lover Donald Himes on Washington Avenue in an elegant Victorian house. Before long he founded the Toronto Dance Theatre with Peter and Patricia Beatty. I went to some of their early concerts at Hart House Theatre and sometimes went backstage to congratulate them. And there were occasional fundraising events, which I attended. One that I remember involved us dressing as Argentinian gauchos and taking part in a tango competition. Exotic stuff for Toronto, even in the mid-'60s.

David continued to dance and choreograph some sixty or more works over the next two decades. I continued to attend his concerts, as well as a great variety of theatre and dance events. One of these was a rather silly musical at a summer theatre in Peterborough, which as far as I can remember was about the tribulations of being a gay dad. Why I went to it I can't recall, but I went to a party afterwards where I met a handsome young actor named Glen

Peloso. He was funny and irreverent, and I found him very attractive. Not too long after, I ran into him again at a restaurant on Church Street where he was working as a waiter. He told me he needed to find some part-time work and was willing to do almost anything. I needed some help cleaning up my workroom and organizing my files. He proved to be very efficient and at the same time amusing. We developed a repertoire of silly banter that included imitations of common friends and the adoption of ridiculous personae. Glen was always fun to be with.

At this time, Judith had developed some health problems to do with her intestinal tract. She was in and out of hospital a good deal, and when she came home she needed a considerable amount of care. I advertised in the paper for a housekeeper and hired a young woman named Anne Ritchie. She was sharp-tongued and attractive and got on with Judith. She became almost like a second daughter. We all got on well but there were underlying tensions. I think Judith resented my developing relationship with Glen, sensing that although we were not having sex together, there was an unstated erotic bond. And Anne, although not exactly homophobic, was somewhat contemptuous of gay men.

I took Glen with me to a concert at the Toronto Dance Theatre's new venue in a reconverted church on Winchester Street and we met David's new lover, Darryl Hoskins, a hunky young man with aspirations to be a choreographer. Afterwards we went out for supper with a few other members of David's company at the Peartree on Parliament Street. David confided to me that he and Darryl were leaving in a month for France, where he was staying at John Syme's chateau near Toulouse. He suggested that I and Glen, whom he assumed was my lover, join them for a week or two.

I had briefly met John Syme in Toronto in the days when he had become something of a countercultural entrepreneur. He began by starting up an alternative art school in a studio on Markham Street. Before long, he had added acting and dance classes at which David Earle taught before the start-up of his own school at Toronto Dance Theatre. John Syme next acquired a broken-down theatre space called the Poor Alex in a lane behind Brunswick Avenue where a number of fly-by-night theatre companies mounted productions with varying degrees of success. Then he bought the Longhouse bookstore, which sold only Canadian books, and moved it from its original Yonge Street location to a storefront in the Annex.

He and his wife Barbara adopted a number of children of mixed race who could often be seen behind the counter of the store or taking tickets at the theatre. But John had always longed to live in France, and so he and Barbara left his various Toronto cultural projects in Toronto to be managed by his children, who slowly ran them into the ground.

When I told Glen about David's proposal, he was immediately enthusiastic about the prospect of a month in France. He pointed out, however, that he was more or less penniless.

I offered to subsidize him up to a point, paying for his airline ticket, hotel bills, and some meals. He was clear that we could not be lovers; he was involved in a long-term relationship with a slightly older actor, Stewart Arnott. I accepted this caveat; I wanted an amusing companion, and I wanted to get away from a home situation where I felt that Judith and Anne were to some extent lining up against me. So we set off and flew to Paris. We spent three days there. I knew my way around and showed Glen the sights. We ate in a couple of good but not excessively expensive restaurants on the left bank and actually ran into two acquaintances, Charles Oberdorff and Gail Singer, which impressed Glen, who obviously saw me as an experienced jet-setter.

We left Paris to drive south in a rented car. Glen was fairly contemptuous of my driving skills and I willingly let him take over, even after he made one or two impetuous moves that might have killed us both. Meanwhile, we spoke in French at his request. My French was limited but serviceable; his was virtually non-existent. Throughout our time in France, he made an ongoing effort, and over time his command of the language increased significantly.

We arrived at John's chateau in the Languedoc and were somewhat dismayed by its appearance. It had no fairy-tale turrets or crenellated battlements, but instead was a decidedly rundown country house, at least half of which was uninhabitable.

John greeted us with enthusiasm. He was a big, hearty Englishman with pronounced buckteeth and a loud and somewhat irritating laugh. He talked volubly while his wife Barbara, who was skinny and faded, provided only the occasional "hmm" on the rare pauses in the John's conversational cascade. She offered us very English meals in the rather disorderly dining room, which like every other room in the house was almost impassable because of the large piles of books that reached from floor to ceiling. We were joined by a healthy-looking English farm boy, who was living with the Symes.

After dinner, while Barbara retired to the kitchen, John took his gnarled walking stick and led us outside to survey his acres. He was running the estate as a working farm and had planted field after field of sunflowers. "Of course I lose money, but the French government subsidizes me. They probably have no idea I'm an Englishman. I've thought of renaming myself Jean de la Syme. Har, har!" His loud laugh rang out across the fields. He led us down a path to the cabin or *gîte*, which I would rent from him for a month. It was neat and tidy, unlike the main house, with a small and simply furnished living room, a well-equipped little kitchen, and a bathroom with an old-fashioned tub with clawed feet and a pedestal sink, whose taps bore the initials "C" for chaud and "F" for froid, confusing at first. There were also two bedrooms with double beds and bureaus but no cupboards. When David and Darryl arrived they would share one bedroom, and Glenn and I would share the other. For the next few nights, however, we would each have our own bedrooms.

A few days later, we drove into Toulouse to pick up David and Darryl at the train station. We settled into the *gîte* amiably enough, in spite of the fact that it rained almost continuously for the next two weeks. Glen and I slept together, and he was not averse to a bit of snuggling and cuddling as long as it did not lead to anything more explicit. I felt a bit like one of those Arthurian knights who places his sword between himself and a damsel to ensure her continued purity.

During the next two weeks, we sometimes went for walks in the rain, sometimes shopped in the local town and visited local restaurants, but mainly stayed home in the evenings. I did most of the cooking, which I enjoyed. Glen and Darryl were much the same age and enjoyed talking dirty together, their banter interspersed with expressions like "fuck me, Mother" and "roll me over and fuck me blind."

Every night at about five, I announced, *"C'est l'heure de pastis."* Glen deprecated my alcoholic tendencies but usually joined us for a libation. In the daytime we visited some of the local towns on their market days and drank in the local ambience, which was still largely uninfluenced by twentieth-century American culture. Then one day David and I went off to see an eleventh-century church nearby and came home to find Darryl in bed with the English farm boy. David didn't fly into a rage. "Boys will be boys," he said and we all settled down for a pre-dinner drink.

A few days later, David and I went for a walk in the sunflower fields. He was no longer the thin stripling I remembered from our youth but had developed a sturdy physique. He had lost most of his hair but he still had huge yellow-grey eyes that dominated his face and seemed to take in everything. We stopped at a certain point and David looked up at me, "I suppose you know I've always found you very attractive." This was not a surprise but I didn't reply. "I don't think it's very generous of Glen to hold out on you. I expect you must feel rather out of it." He then bent his face up and kissed me on the mouth. Inevitably, we were soon on the ground exploring each other's bodies. After half an hour, we had both come and we lay together on the damp ground as it started to rain. "I suppose we should try to clean ourselves up as best we can and go back to the *gîte*." We both took baths, which must have been a bit of a giveaway. Neither Glen nor Darryl made any comments at dinner.

During the next week or so, David and I found a number of occasions to have sex again. I was cast as the aggressor, David as the willing submissive. Certainly we both enjoyed it. I should perhaps have felt guilty, but I didn't. I had realized in my teens that I was attracted to both sexes. I also realized that sex with my peers in high school, in university, and in the Navy was, as the English say, "just not on." There was the odd subversive fumbling, after which I felt guilty as hell, but that was it. But here, away from home, cohabiting with other homosexuals, I thought, "What the hell, I might as well enjoy it while I have the chance."

A week or so later, Glen and I drove into Toulouse. It is an elegant city with a central square surrounded by fine eighteenth-century buildings, including an opera house. In medieval times, the counts of Toulouse were as powerful as the kings of France, and the people of the Languedoc preserve a sturdy independence. They speak a dialect of French, although the old language (*la langue d'oc*) has pretty much disappeared. Glen and I walked around; ate *cassoulet*, a local dish; and wound up in a gay bar. I sat with a glass of wine while Glen investigated the back room. He was gone a long time and I eventually followed him to discover him passionately kissing a blond Frenchman. When he finally reappeared he told me he wanted to stay in Toulouse for a few days with his newfound friend. I told him that was fine by me.

I drove back to the *gîte* and decided to go and visit my brother, who was holidaying with his wife Dorothy in the Dordogne. I arrived at a charming little hotel just in time for an excellent dinner. Bill always seems to find very good hotels that not too many people know about, and this was no exception.

He and Dorothy were excited because they had just learned of the birth of their first grandson, two months premature.

The next day, we drove to Albi and visited the cathedral, which is architecturally unique. It is, in fact, a double church with a splendid late-Renaissance fresco in the apse at one end and intricately carved columns in the second church. We then went to the Toulouse-Lautrec museum. Albi was his hometown and there is a fine collection of his work there in an old chateau. Toulouse-Lautrec is possibly my favourite of all the Impressionist painters, perhaps partly because of his subjects: circus and cabaret performers and prostitutes. This collection contains considerably more of his work than can be seen anywhere else, including the Musée d'Orsay, and I was happy to spend a whole afternoon absorbing the work.

I spent the next day on the dunes outside Bordeaux and returned to the *gîte*, glad to have had a break from its relentlessly gay ambience.

For the next two weeks the rain continued. We stayed in many days. I had brought my portable computer and was working away on some short stories. David and Darryl planned pieces for the next season at the Toronto Dance Theatre. David was by now sole artistic director. He enjoyed the freedom this gave him to create new pieces but found his administrative duties onerous. He talked of stepping down and handing over the artistic directorship to his protégé and former lover, Christopher House. Darryl argued against this, perhaps because he hoped to be David's successor himself. David and I continued to have sex several times a week. We even had a three-way one night with Darryl.

The month came to an end and we all set out for the Mediterranean in my rented car, arriving at Villefranche-sur-Mer between Nice and Monte Carlo, where we stayed in the Welcome Hotel, a small hostelry in a tiny village which boasted a beautiful little chapel decorated by Jean Cocteau, who was one of David's particular enthusiasms. We visited the Picasso Museum at Antibes and went swimming, diving naked off the rocks into the turquoise waters of the sea.

A few days after we arrived, Glen was joined by a Canadian friend called David, with whom he shared a bed. "So much for your monogamous relationship with Stewart," thought I, and in fact Glen and David decided to get married a few months after his return to Canada. We decided on a parting of the ways. Glen and Darryl returned home to Canada while David Earle and I drove down into Italy. We stayed for a day or two in Florence in a disreputable hotel that David knew. It had been a brothel and was still managed by the former madam. The second day she knocked on our door and asked, "*Piace a lei la camera?*"

David replied, "*È brutto.*"

"*Si, è brutto. Mi dispiace.*" She shook her head and retreated. He had meant that it was noisy but had instead had said it was ugly. We received a special discount on our bill.

We picked up Bill Glassco at the Leonardo da Vinci airport on the outskirts of Rome. He had as his companion a young dancer, Michael Conway, who was dying of AIDS, a compassionate gesture typical of Bill. David knew the dancer well. David had also worked closely with Bill at the Guelph Festival under the direction of Nicholas Goldschmidt some years earlier. It was evident we would quickly settle into a compatible group.

I drove directly to the Amalfi coast and made my way along the narrow winding road on the edge of the cliffs high above the Mediterranean. I thought it was a bravura performance on my part.

When we finally reached Ravello, Bill said, "I'm amazed you got us here at all, Martin, but you will not be allowed to drive again on this trip." I was aware not only of Bill's generosity and also of his high-handedness. Very tall and bearded, he looked like a patriarch. He was used to command, having run two theatres, as well as a number of domestic establishments. He was a member of two very high-placed Anglo-Quebec families, and I thought of him as the last of the grand seigneurs.

Ravello is one of the most beautiful places on earth. It has two very good hotels. We stayed at the Palumbo, once a twelfth-century palazzo with a wonderful arcaded dining terrace overlooking the sea. We ate breakfast looking out across the sparkling water glinting in the sun. We then walked in the fabulous gardens, where pergolas with fully blossoming wisteria arched over us. There is a villa in the gardens where Wagner composed *Tristan und Isolde* and another which bears the inscription:

In quest casa la divina Greta Garbo ha passata un settimana d'amore con il gran maestro Leopold Stokowski.

Ravello was also the home of Gore Vidal. Bill, being Bill, had a recommendation from an American college friend (Bill had been an undergraduate at Princeton) who knew Vidal, and we were invited for drinks in the late afternoon. Vidal was charming and, not unexpectedly, extremely acerbic. As we drank Campari and soda, he spoke of the decline of the Broadway theatre, the American political process, and the inevitable approaching downfall of the American empire. He was surprisingly unaffected considering his close association with Washington and the Kennedys, Hollywood, and such stars as Montgomery Clift and Elizabeth Taylor, not to mention Raquel Welch, Mae West, and a galaxy of principessas and contessas in Rome, as well as Anna Magnani, Luchino Visconti, and Truman Capote. After a drink or two I asked him about his friendship with one of my literary heroes, Tennessee Williams, with whom he used to go cruising for young men in Paris. One night when they were unsuccessful, Tennessee turned to Gore and said, "I suppose we could always go back to my hotel and have a go," to which Gore replied, "Don't be grotesque."

Bill drove us down the boot of Italy to Calabria, and we crossed by ferry to Sicily, stopping in the beautiful resort town of Taormina. Bill got us there in record time. He drove very fast and took chances, which I wouldn't have, but I guess he knew what he was doing. I am not vain about my driving skills and willingly surrendered the wheel to him. Our hotel was very grand, with a swimming pool. Michael was feeling weak, so I sat with him by the pool and held his hand while Bill and David made an excursion to Siracusa. We then proceeded to Palermo, arriving on a Sunday morning. We were about to park the car in an almost deserted square when I noticed two guys eyeing us suspiciously. We stayed in the car and watched a guy walking along the other side of the square. A car drove by and he fell to the ground after it passed. The two suspicious-looking characters made a rapid exit. I went over to the fallen man and realized he had been shot dead. Welcome to Palermo.

We stayed in a pleasant rambling old hotel and in the afternoon visited Monreale on a hill above the city and marvelled at its brilliant mosaics. We ate dinner in the hotel that evening, and Bill took over the piano and played a variety of Gershwin tunes. He was an accomplished pianist and rather vain of this skill. David, who hates popular music, went upstairs with Michael, who had eaten almost nothing. The next morning at breakfast, David and I convinced Bill that he should put Michael on a plane back to Toronto as soon as possible. Michael was getting weaker by the day and was concerned that he was going to run out of his medications. We embarked with the car on a boat bound for Naples, drove to Rome, and sent Michael home.

We then drove to the converted farmhouse in Umbria that belonged to Elena Solari, a woman I knew who worked at the Canadian Embassy. We were joined a few days later by Scott Baker, Blair Mascall, and their friend Diana Leblanc. Both Scott and Blair had been students of mine. They were still very good-looking boys, tall and fair and highly intelligent. Scott in particular had been a very promising young actor but after a couple of seasons at Stratford he had decided to become a teacher; Blair, who showed less aptitude for the stage, became an arts administrator. They were already good friends of Bill. Diana was an actor and director, so the conversation revolved mainly around theatrical matters.

We all drove to Pienza, a small town nearby that is off the tourist track and has lovely views. Bill, on a sudden whim, decided he wanted to buy some fine linens. Fortunately I remembered the Italian word for sheet. Once again, we had a splendid meal before we returned to our separate villas. A few days later, Bill drove us to Rome, where he embarked on a plane back to Canada, reluctantly surrendering the keys to me just before he boarded the plane.

David and I set out across the French countryside. David loved France and knew it well. He would often say we should stop and see a certain chapel or garden. At one of these, we were the only visitors, though there were two gardeners working away, a man and a woman wearing big straw hats. At about five o'clock, just as we were about to leave, they asked us to join them for a glass of champagne. They were the owners, a *vicomte* and *vicomtesse*, and they regaled us with gossip about some of their neighbours, who included members of the Rothschild family.

Our goal was the Loire, with its famous châteaux. David was extremely well versed in the history of the late Renaissance, and particularly the early sixteenth century. He had a wonderfully detailed knowledge of court etiquette and the personalities of the period: Henry II and his queen, Catherine de' Medici, and their three dissolute sons, one of whom married Mary, Queen of Scots as a young girl; and Diane de Poitiers, the mistress of the king, to whom he gave the graceful Château de Chenonceau, which spans the Loire, and through which a number of Jews escaped from France to Vichy in the early days of the Nazi occupation. We visited Château de Chambord with its grandiose symmetry; Azay-le-Rideau with its fairytale towers; Château de Blois, which has a spiral ramp inside the great tower so the knights could ride their horses up to the terrace above in safety. The palace itself is still occupied by the family of the French pretender, and his daughter, the Princesse Helene, was married in front of the graceful little chapel dedicated to Saint Hubert, the patron of the hunt. Blois also contains the house where Leonardo da Vinci spent his last years and contains life-sized models of his many inventions, including his flying machine.

We stayed in a number of hotels that were much less grand than the ones we had visited in Italy with Bill. David was full of stories, not just about France, but about his life. He had a lively sense of humour and enjoyed telling about his adventures, sexual and otherwise, which included liaisons of varying duration with many of his dancers. He recalled a party Bill had given at his house on Robert Street in Toronto. The guests were David; Charlie Pachter, the painter; and Scott Symons. They hired a hustler, who danced for them, after which Scott said, "I hope you realize you're entertaining the four most talented artists in Canada." The hustler apparently looked back blankly at them.

On another occasion, David had been picked up in the gardens at Nice by an older man who led him to a grand hotel. The desk clerk refused to give them a room, whereupon the older man revealed that he was a cabinet minister, and the clerk obsequiously showed them to the grandest suite in the hotel. It always surprised me that David's mischievous sense of fun almost never crept into his work, much of which has a strong spiritual content. My brother-in-law, Jamie Cunningham, who had known David as long as I had used to say, "David is interested in high art and low sex." After a good dinner at a local inn, we would retire to our room. We invariably had sex before we went to sleep, and sometimes in the morning before breakfast.

Every day, David wrote in his journal. One day he went out for a walk and left his journal behind. Always curious, I opened it and read several pages. In it he had written that he hoped I would underwrite the work of his company. He also wrote that he found the endless sex wearing and didn't know how long he could sustain it. I realized that I had been very aggressive, even demanding.

I suppose the dam had burst after years of repression. I didn't feel insulted or resentful, but rather glad to know where I stood with David. I backed off a bit in the last few days of our time in France. Back in Toronto, I would continue to see David and sometimes attend his classes. Occasionally we would have dinner and indulge in a little byplay afterwards, but the bloom had gone off the rose.

I found I was glad to be back in Toronto and resume what I thought of, perhaps a bit superciliously, as normal life. I had enjoyed my excursion into gay territory and was happy to have had the experience. It had freed me up and broadened my perspective. It was not that I was shocked by the promiscuity or the shallowness of much of what I had seen, but I was sure I didn't want to join this particular dance, at least as a full-time participant.

I was rather late in coming to terms with my attraction to other men. When I was at school and college, I knew that I was sexually aroused by some of the young guys I knew, but I also knew that if I acted on these desires, I would be ostracized. I also experienced considerable feelings of guilt, probably mainly occasioned by my religious upbringing. Fortunately, I was also attracted to women. Was I a true bisexual? I don't know. I believe that individuals experience sexual attraction in a wide variety of permutations. In any case, I had successful sexual relations with women in the first thirty-five years of my life.

The greater permissiveness of the '60s encouraged me to explore my homosexual inclinations. In the last forty years, I have had a number of pleasurable encounters with other men. As I am not attracted to young boys or indeed teenagers, I have managed to stay on the right side of the law. I have also come to realize that my sexuality was by no means unique. Not only did some of my friends like Bill Glassco share my ambivalent situation, but there were a considerable number of others. This has proved to be a bond shared with people whom I have sometimes known for quite a long time without realizing what we have in common.

In the spring of 2014, my brother-in-law, Jamie, decided to mount a version of the show *From the Horse's Mouth* as part of the World Pride celebrations in Toronto. He asked me to help him, and indeed I raised the necessary money, booked and made technical arrangements with the theatre Buddies in Bad Times, and, with the help of my daughter, Sarah, lined up most of the participants and also much of the audience. He then asked me to participate, and I told a brief story about an early sexual encounter. Jamie felt I was making a valuable contribution towards the understanding of LGBT rights. I doubt the importance of my brief gesture but I didn't mind doing my bit for this cause, although I don't feel particularly strong convictions about it. Jamie has since asked me to collaborate on a book about "coming out" experiences, but it will have to wait until I have fulfilled a good many other commitments.

GOD SAVE THE FOUNDATION

When my father retired at seventy-five, he stopped going to the office on a regular basis but he was still full of beans. He went to the National Club for lunch every day and ate well: veal and ham pie and Waldorf salad in the winter; cold lobster with mayonnaise in the summer, followed by Oka cheese with red currant jelly. In the summer he played golf at the Rosedale Golf Club. He was a mediocre golfer but he had a set of cronies that he played with, and he often took my mother, and sometimes my brother and me and our wives, to dinner there.

For something to do, he developed two projects. He built a large stone house on the edge of a ravine overlooking the golf club. It was somewhat pretentious, with a cupola on the roof and a spiral staircase. It had large living and dining rooms used on the comparatively rare occasions when he and my mother entertained, but he lived largely in the library, which contained few books but a large television set. In the winter, he and my mother went south to resorts such as Pebble Beach in Florida or Sea Island in Georgia. They did not greatly enjoy these holidays. Mother said she only went because she felt Father needed a rest; Father went because he believed Mother needed a change. Often they were accompanied by mother's widowed sister, Bessie, whose sharp tongue provided them with some entertainment.

Although Father had organized his life to his satisfaction, Mother was less contented. Once my brother and I left home, she didn't have much to do. She played bridge once a week with some women she didn't particularly like and volunteered a half-day a week at a hospital, but otherwise she was bored. She was an excellent cook but Father had hired a housekeeper, which meant that she was no longer really at home in her own kitchen. She had all the diamonds any woman could reasonably want, but few occasions on which to show them off. She knew that Father was crazy about her, but although she wouldn't have admitted it, I think she was bored.

Father's second project involved setting up a charitable foundation. He had been an active fundraiser. His particular interest was the Hospital for Sick Children. Every November he would telephone some ten friends and ask them for a donation of ten thousand dollars. In turn, these people would call him when they were canvassing for their pet charity, and he would make out a cheque for a similar amount. But the foundation was a more ambitious effort. He set it up with a generous amount of capital, to which he added every year. He gave money to organizations that interested him, initially mainly organizations that supported medical research. He asked my mother, my brother, me, and our wives to be directors. We met once a year and approved whatever Father had decided to do with a minimum of discussion and then sat down to a hearty lunch. Occasionally, he would question Bill or me about some organization that had applied for funds and we would give our opinion, which he usually acted upon, but our involvement was minimal. Minutes were typed by his long-time secretary Pat Langmuir, who had retired when he did. They were fond of each other and this gave them an opportunity to get together.

Once or twice a month, Judy and I and the children went to my parents' mansion for Sunday dinner. Usually, Mother would have cooked a pie, and we ate in the dining room with its imported lace tablecloth, sterling silver, and Crown Derby china. Mother had always wanted these splendid trappings, but now that she possessed them she had more or less lost interest. My parents were pleased to have grandchildren but made it clear that they disapproved of the way we were bringing them up. However, on these visits the children were reasonably well behaved. Father had installed a swimming pool in the basement of his house, and the children enjoyed swimming in the winter, although Father deplored the mess they made by splashing water on the tiles beside the pool. Both he and Mother were neat freaks, and this left little room for exuberant children to run wild.

It gradually became apparent that Mother was starting to suffer from dementia. All of her sisters suffered from the same condition, but whereas they were happy in their own little worlds, Mother was not. She became increasingly morose and, indeed, vicious. When she started slapping and biting their housekeeper, Father reluctantly installed her in a home. I went to visit her there, and although she recognized me, she cried continually and asked to be taken home. She died of a heart attack after about six weeks. Father felt guilty that he had shortened her life by sending her away. He may have been right, but it is hard to know what else he could have done. He needed the housekeeper to look after him because his eyesight was failing. I felt badly because I never really reconciled with my mother. I knew she had been crazy about me, but we had drifted apart. As a teenager I had felt threatened by her possessiveness and knew that if I didn't get away from her, I would never have a life of my own. She was jealous of my wife and not particularly interested in the personalities of my children. Somehow, I should have reached out to her at the end, but it was too late. She died an unhappy woman.

After her death, I would sometimes drive my father to church on Sunday mornings. I knew that he thought this was good for me. Although he never discussed it, he was upset that neither Bill nor I were regular churchgoers. Sometimes I would stay for lunch afterwards. We would gossip a bit about former colleagues and customers, but as neither of us was much in touch with them, this didn't yield very satisfactory conversations. Then I hit on the idea of playing Scrabble with him. Although this would have been considered sacrilegious when we were younger, it was a happy inspiration. For the next couple of years, he would play Scrabble with me and cribbage with Bill. Father was a brilliant arithmetician; he could add up six or seven columns of figures in his head. Bill had inherited his mathematical ability, which I had not. But in Scrabble, we were not too badly matched. Father was literate and well-read and his verbal skills were impressive. It was also typical of Father that he would assign one game to Bill and another to me. He decided what people were capable of and expected them to live up to his assessment.

I always thought that I was my mother's favourite and Bill was my father's. After all, Father rarely came to see my shows or read my articles. It was only when I advanced this theory to Bill that I learned that he too felt Father rarely took an interest in his athletic or scholarly activities. I think the truth was that Bill was more the person Father would have liked to have been: a jock and popular with his contemporaries, many of whom achieved prominence in the business world. I, on the other hand, was engaged in a number of activities he really didn't see the point of, especially for a man. Not long before he died he said to me one day, "You know, you haven't turned out as badly as I feared you might." It was the highest praise I would ever receive from him.

As my father grew older, he grew weaker and his sight began to fail. He had been diagnosed with glaucoma in his middle fifties and had lost much of the sight of one eye before he was taken on by Dr. Harry McRae, who managed to halt the disease. But in his eighties, he developed a detached retina. He had an operation but was not satisfied with the results and insisted on a further operation, which rendered him almost totally blind. When I spoke to the surgeon, he explained that a second retina operation was almost never successful, but my father was so insistent, he eventually agreed to do it. This was typical of Father, who never accepted that he couldn't get what he wanted until he hit a blank wall. At about the same time, he became almost totally deaf. He could no longer read, watch television, or listen to the radio. It was almost impossible to communicate with him. The last few times I visited, I could only hold his hand and squeeze it. Up to the last, he would squeeze back to let me know he still hadn't given up. When he was finally admitted to hospital with advanced prostate cancer, the doctor asked both Bill and me separately what she should do. We both said, "As little as possible." He died a few days later and, after a private funeral attended only by members of the immediate family, was buried beside my mother in Mount Pleasant Cemetery.

Two or three years before he died, Father handed over the presidency of his foundation to my brother Bill. I was fine with this. I was less interested in the workings of the foundation than Bill was and I readily acknowledged his superior financial skills. When the will was probated, Bill and I discovered that we had each been left generous legacies, but the bulk of Father's fortune went to the foundation. Bill discovered that by transferring Father's securities directly to the foundation, we could avoid paying capital gains tax, thus doubling the value of the foundation's holdings at one fell swoop. During the '90s, Bill managed the foundation's investments and more than tripled the capital. He also handled most of the requests and correspondence. We consulted occasionally and I did some letter writing, but I was somewhat lax and dilatory and at a certain point, Bill confronted me saying, "I regard this as a sacred trust and you seem to think it is just an annoyance. Do you want to carry on with this project or not?" This stung me but also smartened me up and I became somewhat more diligent.

Bill continued to do the bulk of the work, managing the foundation for about ten years, at which point he said, "I'm tired of this. I think we should just give all the money away." I thought about it and replied that I thought we should keep it going. We had several good projects that we were supporting and I felt we should continue with them. So I offered to take over the presidency of the Foundation from Bill and to do eighty percent of the work he had been doing. He agreed to a two-year trial of this arrangement.

Once I became president, I decided to bring in the younger generation. I invited my daughter Sarah; her husband, Douglas Hart; my son Guy; Bill's daughter, Elizabeth; and her husband, Wayne Giesbrecht, to become members of the board. Although a bit shy to offer opinions at first, they soon began to speak up and our meetings became a good deal livelier — in fact, a bit too much so for Bill's taste. He became particularly irritated with my son Guy, who, perhaps because he is a lawyer, questioned everything and made a number of outrageous suggestions.

However, under my leadership the foundation evolved. My father had listed ten organizations he felt we should support, most of them dealing with medical research, such as the Cancer Society, the Heart and Stroke Foundation, and the Canadian Institute for the Blind. We felt obliged to honour his wishes, but the members wanted to use some of the money for causes that were closer to their interests. Bill came up with the idea of setting up portfolios for which each individual member would be responsible. He would continue to handle the medical portfolio; my son Guy would be in charge of the social service portfolio; Judy and my son-in-law, Douglas Hart, would take charge of the conservation portfolio, which would have a subsection concerned with native affairs dealt with by Bill's wife, Dorothy. Sarah and I would take over the cultural portfolio. We decided not to support appeals in the area of education, which may seem strange, as we had all been teachers, but because we had all gone to different colleges and universities, we agreed that it was up to individual members to support the educational institution of their choice. This worked reasonably well overall, although Guy was always behind in his area, and this, plus his confrontational style, became increasingly irritating to Bill.

Fortunately, Bill came up with a suggestion to minimize further friction. We could split the Foundation in two. We would each take half of the capital. His board would include his wife, Dorothy; daughter, Elizabeth; and her husband, Wayne, and would take over the medical and overseas relief portfolios and contributions to the Presbyterian Church, one of Father's primary interests. I could take over the rest: social welfare, arts, and conservation. My foundation would also retain our connection with SickKids, where we continued support, which Judy had initiated, of a research project. It proved to be a workable solution to what was well on the way to becoming a problematic situation.

Once we were on our own, our support of organizations began to evolve. Instead of just giving a donation to be used in whatever way a particular client saw fit, we began to support specific projects. Thus, our substantial donation to the United Way was earmarked for specific projects, setting up the Rent Bank and the Skills Exchange and then a program called Remix, which trained teenage dropouts in specific skills such as operating a movie camera, recording and editing a CD, or designing teenage fashions. All of these enterprises were successful and it was gratifying to visit them and see them at work. Similarly, we supported a project initiated by the Salvation Army to operate a laundry, which trained street people in skills that they might use in getting jobs in the working world.

In the arts, we supported such ventures as the prints and drawings section of the Art Gallery of Ontario and the young playwrights unit at the Tarragon Theatre. And in our conservation program, we supported research into specific endangered species, such as the black-footed ferret and the blue racer, a particular breed of snake. We continued to fund certain social organizations, mainly hostels, and arts organizations like the Stratford and Shaw Festivals and the Toronto Symphony.

I was ambitious to do something more distinctive in the arts. While I was still writing for *Toronto Life*, the publisher, Peter Herrndorf, established something called the Toronto Arts Awards.

I was on the board briefly and, indeed, our foundation provided funding for one of the awards. But two things about this organization bothered me: first, they spent the largest part of their funds on administration and partying; second, their awards went to people like Robertson Davies, Michael Snow, and Jane Jacobs, people who neither needed the money nor the recognition. In fact, the artists were justifying and providing recognition for the awards, not the other way around.

I decided I wanted to set up my own awards and devise a structure where the bulk of the money would go to the artists, and the recipients would be people who, being at an early stage in their careers, could really benefit from the encouragement and the money. I was perhaps motivated by the fact that I had received an award for playwriting in my thirties (the only award I ever received), at a time when it said to me, in effect: "You have some talent. You should go on to develop it instead of improving your golf game."

I approached Janet Stubbs at the Ontario Arts Council Foundation, and with her assistance, we developed a plan whereby the juries that decided on grants for Ontario artists would make recommendations for our awards at the end of their sessions. The council would, at the end of the year, present us with a short list of candidates for our awards in the six categories that they had established: dance, film, literature, music, theatre, and visual arts. The winner in each category would receive eight thousand dollars. Because it was an award and not a grant, it would not be taxable. It was also not accountable; the recipient could spend the money on whatever he or she thought might advance their work in their chosen profession. I once said to one of the winners, a young composer, "If what you think would help you to develop as an artist is to buy a motorcycle, go ahead." He later said to me, "Guess what? I used the award to buy a motorcycle."

Initially, we thought of the awards as going to "emerging artists," a fashionable designation at the time. But Janet said, "This is a substantial amount of money and it shouldn't be doled out to kids two years out of school. It should be given to artists who have produced a body of work and begun to make an impact in their particular field." And so we began giving the awards to artists more or less in their mid-careers. We paid the Arts Council a very modest fee to cover their administrative costs. We relied on the many artists we knew to sit on our juries without a fee, although we gave them a splendid lunch after the jury sessions, which usually lasted no more than two or three hours. These sessions were usually highly enjoyable and performed the additional function of bringing together the artists with their peers.

I am grateful to the Arts Council for their assistance and cooperation. As a young man, I was enthusiastic when Vincent Massey advocated the setting up of the Canada Council and the use of government funding to encourage and develop the arts. In the mid-'60s, bright shoots of Canadian culture sprouted up all around me. Canada produced Margaret Atwood, Leonard Cohen, Robert Lepage, Michael Snow, Teresa Stratas, R.H. Thomson, and Michel Tremblay, to name a few. Theatres, concert halls, and art galleries were built or expanded in all the major cities. Canadian publishers and alternate theatres suddenly appeared like mushrooms in fertile soil. All this was subsidized by government funding through arts councils not only federally, but provincially. The prospects for a growing and vigorous national culture seemed bright indeed.

Now, fifty years later, the dream seems somewhat faded. Canadian artists have had successful careers and many have become stars in the Canadian and international artistic firmaments. We have major artistic institutions, but our larger theatres, symphony orchestras, and art galleries program mostly the work of artists from other nations, apparently conscious that this is what their audiences seem to want. They do try to offer work by Canadians, but it is often marginal to their activities. The alternate theatres struggle on, as do some smaller music presenters; the Canadian-owned publishers have almost all disappeared or been gobbled up by foreign-owned conglomerates. The Canadian film industry is virtually non-existent.

This is not because enjoyment of the arts no longer exists. The performing arts schools and the universities continue to turn out students who are not merely interested, but proficient as dancers, musicians, draughtsmen, and actors. Their love of the arts is ingrained. Some will win recognition and go on to have successful careers, although the majority will not.

In the early years of public arts funding, I chaired a committee to allocate funds to youth theatre companies. In the first year we had five applicants and funded them all handsomely. Five years later, we had thirty applications and gave meagre grants to ten. The arts councils had by then faced the fact that not everyone who thinks they want to be an artist can be supported by public funds. Their motivation in the future would have to be not, in the words of Noel Coward, "the paycheque at the end of the week," but the pleasure of practicing the art of their choice.

I visited Indonesia in the '70s and discovered that a large percentage of the population — perhaps forty percent — paint, write poetry, or belong to gamelan orchestras or dance companies. They start in their early teens and continue this activity into old age. They do this not for money but because it is part of their life, the way Canadian kids skate or play ball hockey or tennis. I think that Canadians in increasing numbers will follow a similar pattern. There will always be writers and artists and performers who pursue these activities for the pleasure it affords them, whether or not it leads to commercial success.

I have also come to realize that, increasingly, the practice of the arts in this country has become a sort of social work. Most artistic institutions have outreach programs that try to connect with young people, particularly the disadvantaged and minorities. This has been strongly encouraged by the arts-granting bodies, who often tie their grants to evidence of community involvement. It is interesting that many young people who have studied to be artists end up as art therapists, using music, drama, or drawing to help people solve their problems or better understand themselves.

Art and social work are not synonymous and yet many artists' work is shot through with social concern. Think of Margaret Atwood and her environmental proselytizing or Robert Lepage's universalism bridging disparate geographical and ethnic worlds. I believe the Canadian arts will have a significant role to play in increasing understanding across the country and around the globe, whether or not it continues to produce the stars of tomorrow. Nevertheless, I find myself sometimes saying to our arts awards juries, "This is not primarily an award based on financial need, but for artistic achievement."

I do not believe that work in the arts should be a competition like that in the world of sports. The job of an artist is to work at his craft and improve his skills, not to strive for fame and fortune. Perhaps in some ways luckily, neither of these is likely to crown his work in our country. I began my work as an actor as an amateur, and I remain an amateur in the true sense of the word, which is that of a lover of art. Amateurs are looked down on by "professionals," which tends to mean people who get paid. Although I have no objection to being paid for what I do, I have come to distrust the word "professional." If the word has any meaning, it is that you are committed to your art and that you are skilled at what you do. In my experience, the appeal to professionalism is in many cases the last resort of the incompetent and untalented.

In spite of some of these considerations, shortly after we began handing out our awards, I decided we should hold an annual event to celebrate the winners and entertain them and their families and friends, along with some of the jurors, some arts-oriented friends, and Council directors and administrators. These events have most recently been held at the Gladstone Hotel at Queen and Dufferin, which has provided a perfect venue. One of my grander friends admonished me, saying that the event should be held at Massey College, but my belief is that Massey, with its elitist aura, would be intimidating. The Gladstone is funky and accessible, and our parties have become celebrated for the unusual mix of attendants and the feeling of community they embody. Each year my former student and long-time friend Laurie Brown acts as our MC, and another long-time friend and collaborator, Bernard Leroux, produces three- to four-minute videos of all the winners. These, in effect, make the evening, because they actually show what the various artists do in their work.

Although our aim with artist awards is not to pick "the stars of tomorrow," it is very satisfying to see so may of our artists go on to do interesting and important work. We have now presented awards to more than one hundred artists and given out more than three-quarters of a million dollars. The artists all live in Ontario at present, but they have roots in Buenos Aires, Singapore, Port of Spain, Mexico City, and Warsaw. They include blacks, Asians, Latinos, and Aboriginals. Interestingly, 40 percent of our winners have been men and 60 percent women, which seems to put paid to the idea that the arts, at least in Ontario, is dominated by the male sex. We have been consistently ignored by the media, perhaps partly because we have not courted them with booze and flattery. In our current media world, you must be famous or rich or both. You are either Lady Gaga or you are nobody. Frankly, I'd rather be nobody.

In all of this work, I have enjoyed a close collaboration with my daughter, Sarah. We each chair three of our juries, and she helps make the arrangements for the event. She has also become the principal administrator of the work of the foundation, setting up interviews with applicants, visiting the premises of various recipients, and sometimes, when she is not satisfied with the work they are doing, cutting them off from further funding. It is gratifying to me to know that she will be able to carry on the work of the foundation when I am not able to do so. And it is also gratifying to see our money in action. Although we have moved some distance from what my father initially envisioned, I think he would be pleased with the way his foundation has developed and the work it is making possible.

LOVERS AND MADMEN

Some time in the '50s, Bill Glassco acquired from a distant relative a country house at Tadoussac at the mouth of the Saguenay River. It had been built in the late nineteenth century by an aide-de-camp of one of the Governors General. It faced the St. Lawrence River, which at that point was several miles wide. In the summer, whales dived and frolicked in the water, and large ships passed frequently on their way to the port of Montreal. The house itself was large and rambling, with several reception rooms on the main floor furnished with Quebecois country furniture, and it showcased many fine examples of habitant wood carving, which Bill had collected over the years. Upstairs were spacious bedrooms and a bathroom featuring a brass tub and shower dating from the early years of the twentieth century. There was a large kitchen with an AGA stove and a good deal of early Portneuf pottery. Bill was extremely proud of his Quebec ancestry on both sides. The Glasscos were a Scots family prominent in Montreal for several generations, and his mother's clan, the Prices, were paper and lumber barons centred in Quebec City. L'Édifice Price is still the tallest building in the old city.

Every summer in August, Bill hosted an extended house party. The house could sleep as many as twenty people, and the assembled guests were mostly theatre people, leavened by a few academics. They were largely Anglophone, but many spoke passable French. One of the necessary qualifications for this party was an ability to cook to a fairly high standard. Bill himself was not a cook, although he occasionally offered to make "my world-famous risotto," provided somebody else would chop the onions.

Every evening there was a splendid meal prepared by two or three cooks, washed down by carefully selected but relatively inexpensive French or Italian wines. Bill, though generous, had a frugal side, which surfaced unexpectedly in certain areas.

One summer, Bill phoned me to say that he would like to invite our old friend Tony Bourne, then living in Victoria, for a week at Tadoussac. Would I be willing to go halves on Tony's airfare, as he hadn't a bean? I agreed, and Judy and I picked up Tony at the Montreal airport. He talked a blue streak on the three-hour drive. I have noticed that people like Tony who live alone explode into conversation when they are with other people. He thoroughly enjoyed his week at Tadoussac, although we took shifts to mentor him in order to avoid being talked to death. Activities included long walks, swimming in a large pool about ten minutes' walk from the house, coffee at a little café in the village, a boat ride out into the river to watch the whales, and picking wild blueberries and gooseberries. In the late afternoon, we cooked. I made a fish stew one night and, on another, summer pudding, one of my specialties.

I knew several of the other guests, including Mary Kerr, a designer I had worked with when she was just getting started, who was a favourite colleague of Bill's. Her designs were stunningly colourful and original but often difficult for actors to wear or work with. Graham Harley once said to me, "If there were such a thing as design police, Mary Kerr would be behind bars." But she was a pretty and vivacious young woman with a ready wit. Another guest was young Nicolas van Burek, son of Bill's sometime collaborator, John. Nicolas was an attractive fifteen-year-old, but he had to be sent home when he fell into the clutches of the town prostitute. There was a lesbian couple, who were excellent cooks and did far and away the largest share of food preparation and shopping, and young Michel Marc Bouchard, who had not yet made his name as playwright but was being mentored by Bill.

There was another aspiring playwright, Jim Bartley. Jim had been a student of mine and we had remained on friendly terms. He was working on a play about Oscar Wilde, who had visited Toronto in the 1880s, at which time he was accompanied by a black manservant. I read Jim's play and expressed interest in it, but Jim told me he was committed to giving Bill the first production, as he had done a great deal to help him shape the play. It was to be produced in Saskatchewan the following winter. I suggested to Bill and Jim that an actor I had worked with extensively in radio, Donald Carrier, would be excellent as the young Wilde, and indeed Bill auditioned and cast him in the role.

After two weeks, we drove Tony to Montreal to catch his plane back to the West Coast. The traffic was heavy and I was afraid we would not get to the airport in time but we made it by a narrow margin, thank goodness. I had enjoyed reconnecting with Tony again but I did not want him on my hands in Toronto.

About this time, John Buchan, the son of my old friend Diane Polley, was just beginning his career as a casting director. He gave me the script of a play he thought I might be interested in. It was called *Molly Wood*, and was about a nineteenth-century Toronto mayor who was gay. I didn't take to it and passed it along to Ned Vukovic, a young director who had established a small but ambitious company under the name of Square Eight. Ned had the bright idea of producing the play with an all-male cast. There was a good deal of doubling and many of the actors took on female roles. It made a strong statement about the gay sensibility in an earlier time. It attracted a good deal of attention and won several Dora awards, partly because the competition in its category was not very strong, and it put Ned on Toronto's theatrical map.

I had become quite friendly with Ned, who was a beer-drinking, cricket-playing Englishman in spite of his Serbian ancestry, and we started getting together for a drink on a regular basis. He had produced *Molly Wood* at the Bathurst Street Theatre, a former church that had been rather crudely converted to a theatre. He had been offered time in the next autumn for a ridiculously low sum. The woman who was managing it wanted something to be produced in the space, but there were no other takers.

Jim Bartley came after me to see if I was still interested in *Stephen and Mr. Wilde*. He felt the play was about Toronto and should have a production here. It was already in rehearsal in Ottawa and perhaps I could bring that production to Toronto. Ned and I decided we would do a two-play season at the Bathurst: Jim's play followed by a revival of *The Misfits*, a play Ned had co-written with a partner about Montgomery Clift and his relationship with Bessie Mae, a.k.a. Elizabeth Taylor. Donald Carrier would play both Wilde and Clift (a role he had created earlier under Ned's direction), with Ned's wife, Lindsay, as Bessie Mae. I agreed to bankroll the season, as I was flush with my recent inheritance.

I went up to Ottawa to see the production at the Great Canadian Theatre Company, which I thought quite good. But when I applied to Equity for permission to bring it to Toronto, they decreed that all the actors must be paid living allowances. This would be prohibitively expensive. So I told them I would do my own original production, though using three of the original Ottawa actors: Don; his beautiful wife, Anaya; and the black Montreal actor Tyrone Benskin. As they knew their lines and I adopted a similar set to the one they had used in Ottawa, I was able to get the production up with only two weeks of rehearsal, even though I recast the three other actors.

Opening night was a huge event. We anticipated an overflow audience, and Equity allowed us to use the seats in the balcony for this one night only without changing the category of the house. It seemed that everyone I had ever met turned up, and had we charged admission we might have broken even on the production. But we didn't have the box office capacity to handle such a big crowd, and anyway there is a kind of tradition that theatre people get in free on opening night. The crowd was enthusiastic, and Kate Taylor gave us a positive review. We did good business, although we never again filled all the seats. Ned was able to rehearse some of the overlapping actors during the run of *Stephen*, and we opened *The Misfits* on schedule. The notices were mixed and one reviewer wrote that we should have used the money we made on *Stephen* to pay for a better set for *The Misfits*. So much for critics' knowledge of the economics of the theatre. But we did reasonable business and the season did a good deal to boost Don Carrier's reputation as an actor.

Ned and I wanted to keep Lovers and Madmen going but we did not have the financial resources to mount another season at the Bathurst. Meanwhile, another opportunity opened up. Damiano Pietropaolo's brother Domenico, who was a professor of Italian literature, took over as head of the Drama Centre at the University. He invited me to lunch and asked me if I might be interested in directing in one of their two small theatres. He could not offer me a salary but there would be a small production budget. The Drama Centre had abandoned Hart House Theatre, but he felt theatre production was an essential component of the Centre's work, if only so that the students had some experience of how a production actually took shape and came together. The Centre was no longer attracting many students who were interested in practical theatre work, but there were a few. He introduced me to one of these, a young woman named Jennifer Smith.

Jennifer proved to be very bright and attractive and we immediately hit it off. She had quite a bit of experience both acting and directing as a student at Dalhousie on the East Coast. We decided to mount a production of *Twelfth Night* at the Glen Morris Studio, with Jennifer both playing Viola and acting as co-director. We held auditions and assembled a cast of young actors, mostly beginning professionals. This is one of my favourite plays. I had directed it before with a slightly less mature cast, but this time the production achieved a balance between the comic characters and the young lovers. Sean Reycraft made a delightfully silly and rather pathetically loveable Sir Andrew, Mary Francis Moore was a pert and lively Maria, and my old friend Rex Southgate gave the performance of his career as Sir Toby Belch — capricious, mischievous, and swaggering. Rex had great difficulty remembering his lines and the other actors never knew quite what he would do or say next, which gave the comic scenes a great sense of spontaneity. The romantic scenes between Viola and Michelle Martin's Olivia had both sensuality and a certain desperation, and gave the romantic part of the play some emotional heft. Jennifer was slight and delicate and in no way very masculine, which accentuated the improbability and pathos of the slightly older woman's infatuation. We used music, which my nephew Ben Stein provided, re-orchestrating original settings of the traditional tunes associated with the play.

Domenico was delighted with the production and asked me to attend a seminar he was giving on theatre production and talk to his students about our show. They were bright and responsive, and I found this a pleasant experience. Afterwards, he again took me to lunch and asked me what I would like to do next. I had for some time wanted to mount a production of Ibsen's *The Wild Duck*.

I had played Hjalmar in a student production directed by Robert Gill, with Hal Jackman as Gregers; a beautiful young woman, Aileen Kamins, as Gina; and Molly Golby as Hedvig. It was a strong cast, but Gill was ill and missed a good many rehearsals and we never really nailed it.

I had two or three actors I wanted to work with. I had also decided that the first act, involving a dozen old men, was unnecessary so I cut it and moved directly to the loft apartment of Gina and Hjalmar. This time I mounted it as a full Equity production in conjunction with Lovers and Madmen.

I financed the production, and although I had some very good actors, including Glen Peloso, John O'Callaghan, Rex Southgate, and Gordon Jocelyn, the production was not entirely successful. Both Glen and John played their roles of the two young men to infer an unspoken homosexual attraction between them. There was no physical manifestation of this but it was palpably there, as the seminar with the students made clear. The Ibsen scholars on the staff must also have picked up on it and they roundly condemned the production.

Domenico suggested that my next effort should be a production of *Galileo*. The idea of producing this great play had considerable appeal. I had already directed several Brecht plays in my time at Hart House Theatre, and I set about working on my own version of the script, using several translations of the various versions of the text. I asked Luella Massey, the Drama Centre administrator, to check the rights and was told that they were tied up worldwide for the foreseeable future. I then thought of asking Pia Kleber of the University College drama program to see if she could intervene, as she had a direct connection with the Brecht family, but I was informed that she was away on sabbatical. I had seen *Galileo* as a good role for Ned Vukovic, and I began to cast about for another play for him. I had for some time wanted to direct *Othello* and that seemed an ideal choice.

Again, this would be a professional production and I sent out a casting call. Within a few days, Thea Gill turned up to read for Desdemona. She was a tall, somewhat lanky blond beauty with an air of innocence, and I cast her immediately. A handsome young stud named Tim Campbell seemed an ideal choice for Cassio. Then, on the last day of casting, David Ferry appeared. I knew his work as an actor and was flattered by his interest. I told him if he was interested in playing Iago, he didn't need to read; the part was his. So I had an excellent cast and we began to rehearse.

Both Ned and David proved a handful. Being directors themselves, they offered more suggestions than I wanted, although I have always believed that I should listen to any suggestions that other people make. I can't expect to have all the good ideas. However, both Ned and David would come to me and say, "You're not going to let him get away with that, are you?" I decided to deal with this head-on. "Tomorrow, the rehearsal is just between the two of you. You will come in at eleven and work your scenes. I will not be here. I will come in at two o'clock and you will show me what you have agreed upon." After that, rehearsals went more smoothly.

I was pleased with the production and we drew good houses. Antoni Cimolino came to see the show and told me, "I've seen three *Othello*s this year and yours is far and away the best." He hired Tim Campbell to work in the Stratford company on the strength of his performance as Cassio. The critics, however, complained that Ned, who was swarthy of appearance and played the role as an Arab Moor, was not black. Political correctness had taken hold and we were among its early victims.

Shortly after this production, I was approached by Anne Tait, who had written a script about the poet W.B. Yeats, a project that she had been working on for some years. She revised it at my suggestion as a two-hander for Yeats and the love of his life, Maud Gonne, and she wanted me to direct and co-produce it. I was able to persuade Domenico to let me use the Robert Gill Studio at no charge, and we mounted it there, with Donald Carrier and his wife, Anaya Farrell, as the romantic lovers. They were well cast: Anaya was an impetuous beauty who could summon up the hauteur of an English aristocrat, and Don had the lyrical sensibility to do justice to the Yeats poems embedded in the text. Anne was a perfectionist and gave the actors many notes, including after the final performance. We played the show in Toronto and toured it to Orangeville and London. My former student Reed Needles was teaching there and agreed to bring his students to the show if I would come and speak to his class. I was happy to do this and was delighted to find that Reed's sixteen-year-olds absolutely adored him. Like all the productions I directed in this period, the play lost money, but as Anne said, "Isn't it satisfying to know you're doing something really good?" This was no doubt meant to compensate me for the twenty-five thousand dollars I had sunk into the production.

A few months later, Ned approached me to see if I wanted to direct him and Louisa Martin in a comedy entitled *Two* at the Factory Theatre. This play was a collection of relatively short scenes involving two characters, a man and a woman, in various unrelated situations in modern-day England. Louisa had succeeded in obtaining the performing rights for Toronto, which was regarded as something of a coup. We began rehearsals and, early on, Ned started giving Louisa directions. I intervened, telling Ned that he was perfectly within his rights to make suggestions to Louisa but not to give her outright commands. From then on, Louisa saw me as her champion and rehearsals went fairly smoothly.

The show was well attended and received favourable notices. Louisa was a pretty woman in her forties and the wife of Lewis Baumander, a director who invariably cast her in leading roles in all his productions, including Gertrude in a *Hamlet* in Winnipeg with his former student Keanu Reeves in the title role. However, Lewis was no longer in great demand as a director and Louisa was languishing. She asked me several times if I would take her out for lunch, and I agreed. She was looking for a challenge and I suggested she might try to sell real estate. She took a course and before long established herself as a successful saleswoman. She then began hosting me for lunch. However, when I sold my house in Rosedale and did not list it with her, I never heard from her again.

In his final year at the Drama Centre, Domenico asked if I could direct a show that involved at least some student participation. I opted for Tennessee

Williams' *Camino Real*. It is to Williams' oeuvre what *Peer Gynt* is to Ibsen's, the mythological base from which all his more realistic work derives. I had done the play once before with my Youtheatre students — not a good choice because all the characters in the play are past their prime and disillusioned. I was able to get some of my long-time actors to take major roles: Rex Southgate, Bie Engelen, and Gordon Jocelyn. I also found a very good youngish actor, Aaron Berg, to play Kilroy.

In the end, the production was satisfying, but it was hell to rehearse. I had a student stage manager; when I asked him to sweep the floor because some of the actors were performing in bare feet, he said, "Sweep it yourself." Meanwhile, he was openly carrying on an affair with one of the actors. The student actors — many of whom had a job (or maybe two jobs), a live-in partner, and perhaps a kid as well — would often say, "I don't know whether I can come to rehearsal tomorrow or not." In the end, it all came together, but not before I had blown my stack and told the actors off. They responded by saying, "We don't have to take that crap from you. Either you apologize to us or we won't do the show." I apologized. I also realized I no longer had the forbearance to direct a student show. In any case, Domenico's term was over, and the incoming director of the Drama Centre had no interest in having me direct in his theatres.

I had written for radio a script roughly inspired by Brian Johnston, who, after a brief stint as drama critic for the *Globe*, was sent to China as an Asia correspondent and wrote a number of sensational articles, including a denunciation of child prostitution in the Far East. He was then profiled in *Saturday Night*, where it was revealed he was running a brothel in the Philippines. I thought this was interesting material and my play, set in Thailand with imaginary characters of course, appealed to several directors. Jordan Merkur agreed to direct it and we found a slot in the Berkeley Street Theatre upstairs. He set about casting it and then suddenly decided he didn't want to direct it. I suppose he decided the material was just too controversial. I then approached Ned, who was happy to take it on.

The cast included Booth Savage as the older guy who had taken up with young prostitutes and a very young Nicolas van Burek as his young protégé. Three Asian actors, Marjorie Chan, Diana Tso, and Arthur Ng, rounded out the cast. We had an exotic set designed by Stephan Droege and a soundscape executed by Richard Feren. The play opened to an audience of mainly theatre people, who were enthusiastic. We continued to get good houses, including quite a few Asians and a good many gays, who commented on it favourably, although the play had no specifically gay content and might have been seen as a derogatory comment on Asian mores. However, the reviews were negative, led by Kate Taylor, who excoriated Ned and me for our voyeuristic and indeed sadistic attitude towards Asian women. After the play closed, I received a letter from the lawyer who represented the writer who had originally exposed Johnston in the press, abjuring me to "cease and desist." As no one ever expressed any further interest in this play, it was easy to comply with this injunction.

While Ned was paid for his activities with Lovers and Madmen and I was not, I was conscious of his need for income. He lived in a two-room apartment at the Performing Arts Lodge with his wife and two daughters and rarely had money for beers, let alone any other luxuries. He did make some money doing voice work and coaching actors, particularly for accents. Briefly, he had a gig at Solar Stage, a small downtown space in the Scotiabank building, where he produced lunch-hour theatre. I directed two productions for him there: a double bill of Tennessee Williams plays, *This Property is Condemned* and *Talk to Me Like the Rain,* with Marjorie Chan and Peter van Gestel. The designers Chris Abrams and Liisa Repo-Martel gave us a clever set. We played to small houses and got a somewhat favourable if patronizing review from Robert Cushman in the *Post*. But Ned wanted something more popular and suggested a play about Eddie Cantor written by Aviva Ravel, who it turned out had been beaten out when I won the drama award for *Out Flew the Web*. We met, and I discovered she was still smarting from the remarks with which Robertson Davies had dismissed her play in the competition.

I hired the actor who had played the Eddie Cantor role earlier in Montreal and a Toronto actor, Scott White. Our manager told me, "You can't hire him, he's obviously gay." I countered, "Yes, but he can play the piano in the style required by the script." The show was a great success with the capacity audiences of aging Jewish women, who commented, "Aren't those two boys adorable. I'd like to take them home with me."

Soon after that Ned got an appointment to teach at the University of Victoria. I was happy for him, because at last he had a full-time job at a decent salary. This meant the end of Lovers and Madmen, but as it had already cost me several hundred thousand dollars, it was probably a good thing. At about this time, I received a notice from the federal government that I owed them a hundred and thirty thousand dollars in back taxes. My accountant, Arthur Gelgoot, had been deducting my production expenses against my investment income. He hired a clever lawyer to contest my case and we eventually had a preliminary hearing. After some dispute, the government lawyer bought my argument that we had been trying to start a professional theatre company. We settled out of court for about fifteen thousand, and another fifteen thousand went to the lawyer. It was a victory of sorts, but it taught me the government was not particularly partial to people who subsidized the arts.

Ned enjoyed his teaching gig in Victoria. For the first time, he and Lindsay and their children had a proper home. But three years later, he developed Lou Gehrig's disease. Lindsay went with him to classes and interpreted as his speech became more and more slurred. Eventually, he had to be institutionalized and she returned to her native England. Bill Glassco was diagnosed with cancer of the throat. He gave up his Montreal apartment and returned to Toronto. His daughter, Briony, nursed him through his final illness and organized a splendid memorial to him at the Royal Alex, which was attended by everyone in the theatre world. Tony Bourne remained in Victoria and at the age of eighty published a book of poems, which impressed me even though I found many of them utterly impenetrable. An inveterate smoker, he died of lung cancer a few years later. A few years earlier I learned that Robert Troop had suffered a fatal heart attack in London and my childhood acting companion Powell Jones succumbed to pleurisy after an operation to replace one of his hips. My artistic cronies were fast disappearing.

NO FOOL LIKE AN OLD FOOL

In the '90s, the Spa on Maitland operated as a male brothel. It had a bar, which at the time none of the other local bath houses did. A collection of young hustlers hung out there offering their services for forty dollars a pop. They sometimes sat at the bar clad only in a towel, sometimes cruised the hallways in their underwear. I would visit the Spa perhaps once a week, usually just after lunch. Several of the hustlers were French-Canadians and it amused me to try out my French on them and try to pick up the current Montreal street slang. I soon learned the terms for cock, ass, and blowjob.

One afternoon, I was approached by a boyish-looking kid with a snub nose and heavily gelled hair called Jay. After a twenty-minute session, I bought him a drink and learned he was a film student at Ryerson. He was obviously bright, with a well-developed sense of humour, which is to say he laughed at my jokes. We began meeting for lunch at a Thai restaurant on Yonge Street. I showed him a film script I had written called *Smarties* about a young bisexual guy from Toronto who forms a liaison with Bohemian young woman in Montreal. It was a light comedy, which moved back and forth between the two cities. Quite a few scenes took place in the bright yellow convertible the hero drove back and forth between the two cities.

At this time, I had become friendly with Sean Hewitt, an actor of about my age who was ambitious to be a film producer. He had a small apartment in the Village in New York and he suggested we make a deal; I could stay at his place in New York if I would let him bunk in one of the bedrooms on the third floor of our house on Sherbourne Street. This proved a satisfactory arrangement. I introduced Sean to Jay and they seemed to hit it off. Jay told us how he had been a child actor in Hollywood. He seemed to be on more or less intimate terms with a number of young actresses, including Drew Barrymore and Alicia Silverstone. Sean said he believed he could raise some funds if Jay could bring either of these actresses on board.

At the time, I had agreed to sit on the board of Theatrefront, a young acting company that was composed mainly of graduates of the theatre program at Queen's University. The group was led by a young director Daryl Cloran. He read my script and agreed to take the project on. He proceeded to do a rewrite of the script with Sean, unbeknownst to me. I was to learn that in the film world, everyone who gets their hands on a screenplay immediately sets about rewriting it: directors, producers, actors, designers, even makeup artists. During the next two or three months, Jay negotiated with several Hollywood actresses, with whom he professed to have connections. He insisted that he alone could handle these delicate negotiations.

A month or so later I had a call from Jay's girlfriend. He was in jail, having been accused of theft by his employer at a ride on the midway at the Canadian National Exhibition. He was shortly released on bail by an uncle. We met and he confessed that this was the second time he had been accused of fraud. He had organized a trade show, which had fallen through, and some of the investors he had attracted had sued him. The case was pending and he needed three thousand dollars to pay his lawyer. I loaned him the money, realizing I would never see it again, but I wanted to help him out. Meanwhile, his negotiations with Hollywood starlets had come to nothing. Sean returned to New York, and Daryl got on with directing a stage show for his young company. Soon after, Jay asked me if I would use my credit card to rent a car for a few days so that he could move with his girlfriend and his dog to Montreal. The next month, I was presented with a bill by the rental company for four thousand dollars. Jay had kept the car for a month and bashed in one of the fenders before finally turning it in Montreal.

I thought I had heard the last of him, but in fact this was just the beginning. I received an email from him informing me that he had dreamed up a reality show related to hockey. The future of television lay in the direction of reality shows, he was certain, which were just coming into prominence with the emergence of *American Idol*. No one had thought of extending the genre to the world of sport. Would I be interested in helping him realize his vision? The potential profits could be enormous. He was returning to Toronto and maybe we could meet. I should, of course, have blown him off but I was intrigued.

I presented Jay's outline to my long-time friend and sometime collaborator Bernard Leroux. He was immediately interested and brought on board one of his associates, David Grein, a film editor and sound technician. We arranged to go to a hockey training camp, where Bernard shot some footage. David edited it and produced a lively demo that gave some indication of the potential of Jay's idea. We then managed to get interviews with the Sports Network and the CBC, both of whom expressed interest, partly because a strike was looming in the National Hockey League. Jay proved to be an effective salesman, setting up interviews and delivering an effective spiel.

Jay's idea was that we should convince Don Cherry to come on board as the chief arbiter and commentator on our projected show. Don agreed to meet with us but proved evasive. Jay then went after Doug Gilmour, who had just retired as captain of the Maple Leafs. He agreed to take part in a shoot. I was able to get a studio at the Drama Centre, and Doug showed up and was an effective on-camera presence. Bernard and David revised and re-cut our demonstration video, interjecting sound from a Nickelback recording. We approached a small advertising agency, who were enthusiastic and helped us set up interviews with potential sponsors, including Campbell's Soup, Labatt, and Frito-Lay potato chips. They all responded with enthusiasm, and we began to think we were really onto something. Then we got an interview with one of the senior advertising executives at Bell Canada. He liked the project and we thought we were in business.

By this time, Jay had moved home from Montreal to Barrie, where he lived with his widowed mother, two sisters, and four-year-old nephew. He felt an obligation to support them and look after them. They, in turn, looked out for him. One day, I had a visit from a lawyer who thought Jay might be living in my house. The lawyer was acting for an aging female journalist whom Jay had bamboozled out of tens of thousands of dollars, as well as a Hollywood scriptwriter who had also "loaned" him a sizable amount of money. The lawyer had already visited the Barrie home of Jay's mother, who told him she had no idea where her son was. In fact, he was shacked up at his mother's house in Barrie with his girlfriend and his dog.

I rented a car for him so he could drive back and forth from Barrie to Toronto and also attend meetings at Dave's office in Unionville, a pretty little town with a couple of good restaurants. Dave took a particular liking to Jay, and they spent some time together going to junior hockey games, supposedly to suss out potential talent. Dave had been a goalie, playing junior hockey in Kitchener. He told me he looked on Jay as the son he had never had. However, he eventually told me that Jay had in fact been in an accident on the Barrie highway, and the rented car was totalled.

I picked up a bill for eight thousand bucks.

Jay talked me into going with him to Banff for their annual TV conference. I was already acquainted with Pat Ferns, the former TV producer who was now the CEO of the Banff conference and he received us graciously. My old friend Laurier LaPierre was one of the hosts, and we were welcomed to seminars and cocktail parties. Jay proved to be an enthusiastic party animal and stayed out most nights till dawn, returning home to clean up and setting out in the morning to schmooze his way through the day. He told me he once flew to Los Angeles just to go to a party. While in Banff, he claimed to have made some valuable contacts before we set off for home.

We had learned in Banff that there was a rival program being developed around the same basic idea. Back in Toronto, I attended a meeting with Doug Gilmour and his wife, and Doug announced he had decided to pull out of the project. He would later tell me privately, "My wife persuaded me that Jay was full of shit." We scrambled around to find another star hockey player and were able to set up the beginning of a deal with Mark Messier, a Canadian playing for the New York Rangers. He was brought on board by a friend of David Grein's who was a sports commentator in the United States. We met with him and agreed to give him a piece of the action if the project went ahead. All of these meetings had to be subsidized, and I laid out money for airfares, expensive lunches, and even hotel accommodation. Mark Messier's participation was negotiated by his sister, who, as his manager, came to Toronto to meet with us. But we learned that Bell had decided to back our rivals and the CBC had picked up their show for airing in the fall when the NHL players were on strike.

Jay made a last-ditch appeal to me, saying that he had managed to land an interview with the producer Jerry Bruckheimer in Hollywood. I gave him money to fly to Los Angeles, and he returned saying Bruckheimer was impressed and would likely come on board. I had set up an account for the project and was prepared to give Jay joint signing powers. Although he never complied with the bank's request for proper identification, they allowed him to withdraw some thirty thousand dollars from the account. He told David Grein that I had withdrawn the money. David and I set up a meeting with him to confront him with his varying stories. He didn't show up. Later that night he phoned to say he was in the Women's College Hospital. He was convinced he had had a heart attack. "I'm scared," he whined. "Can you come and see me?" I went to the hospital, where he was hooked up to a couple of machines. He seemed pallid and exhausted. I stayed for a while and he said, "I'm so grateful to you. You know I love you."

It was now clear that the CBC were going to go with the rival show. It aired in the fall and we watched it avidly for the first two or three episodes. It was a bore, lacking in any real dramatic arc or even competition among the players. Would our show have been better? I couldn't tell, but I knew that after a week or two the ratings dropped drastically. Before long, the strike was settled and the idea of a reality hockey show or any other kind of reality sports show was never revived. One way and another, I had dropped some hundred and fifty thousand dollars on this project. Anyone might have thought I had learned my lesson.

Some months later, Jay came up with a project to do a TV series called *The Publicist*, featuring an aggressive young woman who had a roster of clients that included Moses Znaimer and George Jonas. Jay talked Bernard into covering the woman's activities at several parties. I agreed that Bernard could spend the week at my house and Dave was prepared to do the necessary editing. Meanwhile, Jay was romancing the publicist's assistant, a very pretty Jewish girl. As she was married, a certain amount of discretion was called for, although how anybody could have missed what was going on was a mystery to me. Bernard and I went with Jay to several parties during the Toronto International Film Festival. These were attended by a lot of smartly dressed young people who were there to be seen. They mingled with the crowd, hoping to connect with agents, producers, or visiting stars. Bernard shot a good deal of footage. I tried to interest Jay in doing interviews and indeed did some myself while he schmoozed. When we eventually took Bernard's footage to David, he went through it and said that essentially there was nothing there: no story line, no compelling moments, just a lot of people trying to have a good time. He was not even able to put together a decent demo.

Jay told me he had another film project. He was going to make money and start to pay me back. I had set up a company with him under the name Guardian Entertainment. I consulted a senior lawyer friend who set me up with one of his juniors. He met with Jay and me. In a private conference with me afterwards, he told me that Jay was obviously a con man. It was not as if this was news to me, but I had tried to convince myself that he had real potential if he was just given a chance. Casey, the lawyer, said I should close the company down before I incurred any further losses. We met again with Jay, who refused to give up his position in the company. Casey brokered a deal whereby Jay retained ownership of the company and I would own the rights to *MVP*. They would of course be worthless, but I could claim a substantial tax loss. After the meeting, I went down to the basement of the bank building where the lawyers' offices were located. Jay was waiting for me.

"You know I love you. You've been like a father to me."

"I love you too, Jay, but I don't love the way you act." My words were an echo of something I remember my mother saying to me when I was a teenager. I walked away. When my Visa bill came in at the end of the month, there was a charge from the Four Seasons Hotel for over four thousand dollars. Jay had evidently got the number of my credit card and forged my signature. No doubt he had spent a few nights during the festival there with his Jewish lady friend.

My lawyer son, Guy, was horrified when I related the details of this adventure. He set up a meeting with the Four Seasons manager, who agreed to rescind the charges on my Visa. He explained that during the film festival the hotel was fully booked at rack rates; stars came in the back way, disguised to avoid being recognized; the hotel was full of people, many of them highly inebriated; and the staff had very little control over what went on. Guy next mounted a court case, using the evidence I supplied him. We got a judgment against Jay, demanding that he compensate me for the expenses I had incurred. I thought this was a waste of time and effort, because Jay had no money and probably never would have. And in any case, we would have to find him. We discovered that he had a website which presented him as the inventor of *MVP* and cited some work he had done as a producer on a small Canadian feature titled *Pontypool*. The last time I checked it out, it revealed that he was wanted for fraud in both Los Angeles and New Orleans.

Looking back, it is clear to me that I must have wanted to be conned and cheated, perhaps as a punishment for my homosexual philandering or perhaps to satisfy some underlying masochistic streak in my nature. I remember, back in college, my friend Peter Russell saying to me, "Hunter, I don't understand why you think so poorly of yourself." I don't think I responded, but of course it was in part a holdover from my childhood and adolescence, when I realized that I had not measured up to my parents' expectations and I never would. Because my father measured success in terms of money, squandering a good chunk of the money he had left me must have been in some sense a way of getting back at him.

Motivation has always fascinated me. Perhaps that's one reason I set out to be a dramatic writer. I am sure one of my father's greatest fears was that I would turn out to be what he would have called a pansy. He never spoke of this possibility openly, but only said things like, "I don't know what you think is going to become of you." Towards the end of his life, he may have realized that his fears had not been unfounded, but if so, he never alluded to it.

One of Jay's legacies was to hook me up with a middle-aged Brit called Robert. Robert had worked as a line producer for many years. He was enthusiastic about two of my scripts and asked me to engage him as, in effect, my agent. He would shop my work with his many contacts for a monthly salary. He deplored the state of the Canadian film industry loudly and at length, which I soon found repetitive and boring. I also had to tell him that I couldn't subsidize him indefinitely. He suggested a number of producers and directors, some of whom I knew already.

One of them was Tim Bond, whom I had known when he was a young stage director just getting started. He grew up in Ottawa and began working for Marigold Charlesworth and Jean Roberts, who were then running a small professional theatre. They called him in and said they had heard he wanted to be a director. When he answered in the affirmative, Jean apparently said, "My dear, you haven't a hope. You're not British." Tim went on to work in summer stock and at Stratford, and directed William Hutt and Robin Phillips in *The Dresser* in Vancouver before he went to Hollywood and had a profitable career directing B movies and television.

I remembered Tim as a young man being smart, attractive, and rather arrogant. He hadn't changed greatly but he said, "I get a lot of scripts and this is one of the best I've read in some time. However, I'm a director, not a producer. And anyway, the future of television lies in series, not one-off dramas." I came up with an idea for a Canadian series about three generations of a family at their summer cottage in the Gatineau. I wrote a pilot script and two follow-up scripts. Both Tim and Robert were enthusiastic. Because it was set in Quebec, Tim thought we should seek a Quebec producer. Robert had a connection with a producer named Louis Porco, and I had already a slight connection with another producer, Claudio Luca. We decided to visit Montreal and arranged to set up meetings with both men.

Tim drove, and we arrived in the evening just in time to have dinner with Peter Pearson. Peter and I had been child actors together. He had just retired from a job as chief showrunner for English-language television drama at the CBC. We had a convivial evening, and Peter warned us about Quebecois producers, implying that many of them were in league with the Mafia. The next day, we had good meetings with Claudio and Louis and more or less made a verbal deal with the latter. He was represented in our negotiations by a brisk and capable woman, Marie-Christine Dufour, his vice-president. We returned to Toronto and I got to work on preparing pitch documents under Tim's supervision. We sent them to Marie-Christine, who responded positively but said she would feel more comfortable if we would bring on board a co-writer with more television experience. She would find us someone suitable.

A week later, we were visited by an American woman who was living in Montreal. She gave us a PowerPoint presentation. She then read my script and said, "You'll never sell this. Nothing happens. Your characters are boring. They need to have more secrets." I was somewhat crushed. Two days later, Tim called to say, "I'm sorry, but you're out. I'm going to develop your idea with this new scriptwriter. I will of course make sure you get a royalty. Shall we say one-half of one percent of the gross budget if the series goes to air?"

I was pissed off but realized there was nothing much I could do. Tim's agent, who had expressed an interest in also acting as my agent, called me and said, "I've drawn up a contract. You should accept their terms. Otherwise you will get nothing." Tim went off to Montreal to work with his new writing partner. After a week or two, he reported back to me about their outline. It did not vary so much from my original but was jazzed up, beginning with an explosion, which killed off the wealthy parents who left their children with no inheritance except the cottage. They considered this a much stronger and more saleable premise, and Tim was confident of their ability to pitch it. They obtained meetings with both the CBC and CTV but were unable to make a sale. Tim said we should leave the idea to simmer for a year or two and went off to his house in France with his boyfriend. I retired to lick my wounds and concluded the world of television was not for me. For twenty-five years I had tried to peddle a variety of projects without success. I was used to collaborating but not to being summarily dismissed. Now in my early seventies, I figured it was time to stop kidding myself and turn my energies elsewhere, though I still had one more project I was determined to see come to some kind of fruition.

THE TENNESSEE WALTZ

One day my brother-in-law, Jamie Cunningham, phoned to say he had just seen an excellent play titled *Full Gallop*. He wanted to do it himself. I assumed that he was interested in directing it, but it soon became evident he wanted to act in it. The play was about Diana Vreeland, the former editor of *Vogue* who, upon retiring, set up the costume department at the Metropolitan Museum in New York. The fact that Jamie wanted to play a woman was not a complete surprise. He was an acknowledged homosexual whose work as a choreographer included a good deal of gender-bending.

I read the play and then tried to see if I could obtain the performance rights. I was told that the woman who had written the play intended to go on performing it for some time, and the rights would not be available for several years. I then suggested to Jamie that if he wanted to perform, we should collaborate on a play for him to star in. As a possible subject I suggested Tennessee Williams, a writer we both admired and whose work we knew well.

We immediately began reading everything we could get our hands on by and about Williams. We discovered that there were a good many lesser-known plays and a host of books by people who had known Williams, from renowned authors like Gore Vidal to more obscure writers such as Dotson Rader and Bruce Smith. There were racy articles in such publications as *After Dark* and detailed descriptions of his long-time relationship with Maria St. Just, including many letters and his own sensational *Memoirs*.

As Jamie lived in New York and I was in Toronto, we had lengthy telephone conversations about this material. The following summer, we met at the Cunningham family cottage in the Ottawa valley and set to work mapping out a scenario. It involved Williams hooking up with a hustler at the Elysée, the hotel where he habitually stayed when in New York. At the beginning of our play, Williams is supposedly opening a new play of his own; he refuses to attend the premiere but sits at home waiting for the reviews. He and the hustler while away the time playing poker and swapping stories. The hustler, a would-be actor, gradually figures out his identity as Williams revisits scenes from his past. The other characters are his mother, Miss Edwina; his sister, Rose; his father, Cornelius; Maria St. Just; and his long-time lover Frank Merlo, who appear in flashback sequences. We decided that I would write the scenes with the hustler, Maria, and Frank, and Jamie would write the family scenes involving Rose and their parents.

During the next year, we each wrote scenes. Jamie mailed me his work written in longhand, and I agreed to stitch the various bits and pieces together. I added some lines to some of Jamie's scenes, and he wrote an opening monologue for Williams and added some material to my work. He also vetoed some of my ideas. This was not a surprise. I knew Jamie had strong views on many topics and could be highly critical. Eventually, we arrived at a script that we were both reasonably satisfied with.

The next step was to organize a reading. We assembled some actors that Jamie knew in New York and had an initial session at the apartment of one of the actors' grandmother's in midtown Manhattan. Jamie read Williams, one actress read Maria, another doubled the roles of Rose and Edwina, another actor doubled Frank and Cornelius, and still another actor played the hustler. It read reasonably well and we decided to do a rehearsed reading at a small theatre on Thirty-fourth Street on a Monday evening for about forty invited guests. Although there was some laughter, the comments of some of the audience members were not particularly favourable. One man said he got tired of William's endless kvetching about the critics. Another said the problem was that you got no indication of the brilliance of Williams' work. Both of these comments made an impression on us and stayed with me. Although we spoke to several potential directors who had connections with theatres in New York and Los Angeles, nothing came of them. I could tell Jamie was losing interest in the project. He was no doubt discouraged by his friends' lack of enthusiasm, and he admitted to being daunted at the prospect of learning all those lines. In our play, Williams never left the stage. The project languished.

In his last year as director of the Drama Centre, Domenico Pietropaolo suggested I might do a modern play with a predominantly student cast. I chose Tennessee Williams' *Camino Real*, partly because I had done the play once before with the kids in my Youtheatre company, and I wanted to it again with some more mature actors. Domenico was keen to organize a seminar about Williams, and he put together a panel of academics, chaired by Ronald Bryden, that included me and Diana Leblanc as two experienced directors of Williams' plays. He then said to me, "I understand you have a play about Williams. Couldn't we do a staged reading of it after the seminar?"

I was approached by a mature student, Ed Martin, who agreed to direct the reading. I found three actors: Bernard Hopkins to play Williams; Allegra Fulton to play all the female characters; and Glen Peloso to play all the men. Ed worked with the actors for three days and actually got them up on their feet, though of course they were still holding scripts. The reading was extremely effective, and the audience of some fifty people was much more enthusiastic than the viewers in New York. This was partly because the show was better cast and partly a tribute to Martin's skills as a director. Bernard Hopkins was particularly fine as Tennessee: witty, articulate, and ultimately very moving. I thought Ed might be interested in doing a full-scale production but he suddenly left town. I learned that he was a big-time gambler and presumably he got away just in time. I never heard from him again.

Bernard was enthusiastic about the play and particularly his role. He went to bat with Andrey Tarasiuk, one of the producers at Stratford, who somewhat grudgingly set up a workshop. This time there were seven actors, including some of the senior actors in the company, each playing a single character. There was a small invited audience and they responded favourably. But Richard Monette had decreed that the company would not do one of my plays while he was artistic director, so that was that.

I then came up with the idea that our play could be adapted as a screenplay. Jamie said he was not interested in working on this version but agreed I should go ahead. At the time, I was serving on the board of Tapestry New Opera Works, an organization devoted to the development of musical theatre. The president of the board was a singing lawyer, Conrad Willemse. He read the draft of my screenplay, liked it, and said we should form a company to develop it. He introduced me to David Korchok, a young locations manager with ambitions to become a producer. "David is super keen and has some good contacts. He'll drive the project forward." David was indeed hungry and personable, and we formed a company with the three of us as equal partners.

In order to raise some capital I gave a party for some of my wealthy friends who were interested in the arts. I engaged my friend Bernard Leroux to produce a short video about Williams using some of the many still photographs of the dramatist and brief clips from some of his films. I also brought on board my friend Anne Tait, the casting director for Kevin Sullivan's movies as well as many other projects. We offered our guests drinks and finger food and pitched them on the project. Several signed up for shares in our company at five thousand bucks apiece and we now had capital of fifty thousand dollars.

Now that we had some funds, David suggested he should go to Hollywood to peddle our project. He came back and reported that he had managed to connect with a woman named Candy Walters who was a highly influential broker of scripts with close connections to Paramount Pictures. Unbeknownst to me, David had given my script to his wife, an aspiring screenwriter, who did an extensive rewrite. He reported back that Candy loved the script and it was only when I managed to get a copy of it that I discovered what he and his wife had done. I went to Hollywood and met with Candy, who claimed to be horrified by David's duplicity, although I expect she had seen plenty of similar episodes in her career. She suggested we engage a young writer she knew to give the script a "polish." The script came back to me and I found that what he had done was not an improvement but a distortion. We paid him five thousand dollars and he signed off.

Candy was a middle-aged woman with a gutsy laugh and the air of a sort of rollicking pirate queen. She lived in a pretty little house in one of the canyons, had trained as a lawyer, was a recovering alcoholic, and had a passion for snowboarding. We hit it off and she suggested that she work closely with me on a rewrite. She agreed to do this for an additional ten thousand dollars. We agreed that we would drop Korchok and set to work. Over the next few months, we communicated by email and came up with a script that I do think was stronger and tighter. She agreed to take it to her contacts at one of the studios. We had succeeded in spending over half our capital. We had dumped Korchok but he still claimed to hold a third interest in our venture and Conrad said he had legal rights. We eventually bought him out for fifteen thousand dollars. Candy made what in the trade are known as "best efforts" but to no avail. She was unable to sell our screenplay to a producer who could carry it forward.

Some months later I told Ronald Bryden about the script, and he offered to see if Robin Phillips would read it. He was much closer to Robin than I, although we did have an acquaintance. Robin had expressed interest in one of my earlier scripts. I had interviewed him for the CBC and written about him for *Saturday Night*. He had also asked me, when he was at the height of his power at Stratford, to convene a group of well-known writers with a view to encouraging them to write for his theatre. In attendance were Robertson

Davies and Timothy Findley, both of whom had already written for theatre. Michael Ondaatje sent his regards; Margaret Atwood sent her partner, Graeme Gibson, as an emissary; Alice Munro made it clear she had no interest in writing plays. Robin expressed his thanks to me but, quickly seeing that this scheme was going nowhere, declined to call a further meeting.

Robin, whose career was in the doldrums when Ron approached him, agreed to read my script. He got in touch with me promptly to say he loved the script and would be honoured to work on it as director. He put me in touch with Dick Nielsen, whom I already knew. Dick and I had a lively lunch and he expressed delight at working with Robin and me. He would act as producer. He offered me a two-year contract with no advance. If the project went ahead, he as producer would get sixty percent of the profits, and I would get forty percent, as well as a royalty. There was an escape clause, which would allow either of us to get out of the agreement on two months' notice.

Robin did not ask for a rewrite but rather set to work on a design for the film. He apparently created a model, which I never was able to see, although I met him several times in Stratford at an obscure restaurant where we wouldn't be observed. Robin exerted his considerable charm at these meetings, and he was confident and optimistic. He sent the script to Jessica Lange, whom he had directed in London, and she agreed to play Miss Edwina. I think she thought the project had financing and would proceed shortly. Robin decided to go after Robert Downey Jr. to play Tennessee. Unfortunately, Downey was just starting to recover from a drug addiction and because of his recent misbehaviour on a couple of recent films was uninsurable.

Dick had been confident Robin's name would attract talent of the highest calibre but this did not prove to be the case. The months went by, and there was no real progress in attracting a starry cast or any financing. Robin had proven himself an exciting stage director but his one major film, based on Timothy Findley's novel *The Wars*, had been a flop. A few years later, I would go back to Robin to see if he might be willing to direct the stage version, but he declined, saying he could no longer make himself available for stage work. By this time, his reputation for being difficult had reached the point where I don't think many theatres were willing to work with him.

During the time I had spent at the film festival with Jay, he introduced me to an English director named Don Boyd, who was screening a documentary about a gay English couple the same afternoon. Jay knew about my Williams script. He invited Don to lunch at Sassafraz (for which, needless to say, I paid) and very effectively pitched my script. Don said if I would let him have a copy, he would read it on the way back to England and get in touch with me. I was skeptical about the likelihood of this, but indeed the next week I heard from him saying he liked the script and would be interested in directing it. He would like some revision, of course, but perhaps I could talk to his agent in Hollywood and we could come to an arrangement. The agent said that Don was prepared to work on the script with me if I could go to London. He would need a retainer of ten thousand dollars. I got in touch with Dick Nielsen and informed him I wanted to be released from our contract. He sympathized with my frustration and we did the necessary paperwork.

I set out for London and met Don at the Groucho Club, a haven in Soho for theatre people who could not afford the much grander Garrick Club. Don proved an amiable companion and his ideas for a revision of the script were interesting. I had brought my portable computer with me and set to work each morning where I was staying at Rodney Archer's house in Spitalfields. Don and I would meet every day for lunch, usually at some rather elegant establishment liked The Ivy or Prunier and review what I had written. He was very complimentary about my work and we discussed casting. He saw the older Williams being played by John Hurt, whom he knew. This didn't strike me as brilliant, but when I saw Hurt's earlier impersonation of Quentin Crisp, I began to see the possibilities. After a fortnight, I had completed the rewrite and returned home to wait for developments.

We continued to correspond by email and within a month, Don informed me had found a producer. I should return to London to meet him. Tarquin Gotch was a large, jovial Englishman, and he greeted me with enthusiasm and expressed confidence in the project. Although Don thought that Hurt was prepared to play Williams (Hurt's wife loved the script), we needed to attract some other name actors. What about Judi Dench to play the older Rose and Gael García Bernal as the hustler? There were other names, mainly English, bandied about.

Tarquin felt we needed to get a casting agent on board. He suggested a woman named Celestia Fox, and we met her for lunch. She was a middle-aged, gap-toothed siren who had once been married to one of the acting Fox brothers. She agreed to take on the project for ten thousand dollars. Over the next few months, partly at my suggestion, we pursued a number of American actors: Christina Ricci agreed to play young Rose, depending on who would be playing the young Tennessee. Frances Conroy was prepared to play Miss Edwina. But we still had no one to play the young Tennessee. Celestia pursued Macaulay Culkin, who reported that he liked the script but wasn't prepared to play yet another gay character. We had the beginnings of a "package" but lacked someone for the crucial role of the young Tennessee.

Tarquin went to Hollywood to talk with some producers he knew. They had suggested various young stars, but none of them wanted to play an openly gay character. John Hurt let it be known that he had other offers. Eventually, Tarquin reported back to me that he had been unable to sell Don Boyd as a director. The project needed somebody like Stephen Daldry or Gus Van Sant. I asked him if he could approach either of these directors and he replied he would see what he could do.

Meanwhile, Don heard of his disloyalty and was understandably furious. I don't know if the two men had it out, but it became apparent that Tarquin had more or less given up on the enterprise. I think the truth was that Tarquin had made a good deal of money working in the American music business, married a young wife, started a family, bought a substantial house in the English countryside, and wanted to settle down and just enjoy life. In any case, the emails between Tarquin, Don, and I gradually grew more and more infrequent and I had to realize nothing was going to come of our collaboration. I moved on to other projects.

I had become accustomed to going to England at least every other year, but after my experience with Don and Tarquin, the incentive lessened. My friend Robert Troop had died suddenly and my friend Dick Williams had moved to a remote corner of Wales. Another good friend, Liz Bluhm, the adoptive mother of my wife's niece, Annika, had also died. When my brother, Bill, suggested we should go to Italy together one last time, I agreed. I would spend a few days in London first because I wanted to see my friend Powell Jones, who was ailing. Sadly, he died two days before I arrived in London. I visited Robert's widow, Liz, and found her rather morose and diminished. Bill and I flew to Rome and drove to Orvieto, where we stayed at a *fattoria* that took in tourists. We ate delicious food and drank the crisp white wine of the region. We visited Gabriele at his Trattoria dell'Orso. He cooked us a special pasta dish and sat down and ate it with us, congratulating me on becoming a famous author. I saw no point in disillusioning him.

Bill and I then proceeded to Florence, where we stayed at the Porto Rosso and hung out with our good friend Jim MacDougall. Jim had been a classmate of Bill and my brother-in-law Jamie at University of Toronto Schools. He had trained as a physician, studied tropical medicine in London, and then agreed to go to Nairobi for a year to help set up a clinic. In fact, he had stayed for twelve years. Judy, the kids, and I visited him in Kenya one summer, visiting the game parks of the Serengeti and Keekorok, the Ngorongoro gorge, and Mount Kilimanjaro. We saw lions and giraffes and elephants and the tribal dancing of Masai warriors. We spent ten days at a resort on the coast north of Mombasa. Most of our luggage was stolen and we were bumped off a plane, but in spite of that, it was a wonderful trip.

When Jim returned to Canada, he decided he had had enough of being a doctor and devoted himself to his real love, painting. He became a highly accomplished portraitist and every year spent a month in Florence, studying and painting models. Jim took us to restaurants we would not have discovered otherwise and pointed us to some of the lesser-known churches to see frescoes by obscure Renaissance painters. Quite by chance, I ran into David Ferry, who was directing a play at a small theatre on the outskirts of the city.

We met for lunch, in the course of which I told David I had this play about Tennessee Williams. He agreed to read it.

A month later, back in Toronto, David and I had lunch again. He told me he thought the play had distinct possibilities and that he might agree to direct it if I were prepared to rewrite it from top to bottom. He thought the female characters were the most interesting, with the exception of Tennessee. I had got used to rewriting when I wrote scripts for the CBC and agreed to accept his terms on the condition that he give me specific guidelines. I went back at the script. I eliminated Maria, Frank, Cornelius, and the plot about the opening of a new show. The whole script was to be like a dream that Tennessee might have on the last night of his life.

The Hustler, who appeared unbidden outside the window of his hotel room, was to be the catalyst who invoked the past, and he would briefly assume the personae of the other men in Tennessee's life. We arranged a reading of the new script with Bernard Hopkins, Diana Leblanc as Miss Edwina, Laura de Carteret as Rose, and Mac Fyfe as the hustler. David pronounced the play a big improvement, although not yet completely ready for production.

I had become involved with Hart House Theatre, which was coming to life again after a hiatus of thirty years, during which it had become largely a rental facility. Doug Floyd, the new manager, perked up his ears when he heard I had the interest of David Ferry, who had recently had several successes as a director. He offered to include my play, now re-titled *The Gentleman Caller*, for a week's run in the fall of his 2011–12 season. He offered me the theatre rent-free and would handle the advertising and box office, since the theatre was set up to do this, though I would have to finance the actual production. 2011 was the centenary of Williams' birth. It seemed to me the pieces were coming together and that this was an offer I couldn't refuse. We established the dates and David agreed to take on the direction.

There were, however, difficulties. Bernard Hopkins was keen to do the show but he was now physically incapacitated. He had a heart condition and could barely walk. His caretaker informed me that he would not permit him to play in the show. Diana Leblanc was also unavailable because of other commitments. And David had belatedly joined the Stratford company, replacing Peter Donaldson after his death. David said we would have to cast the show with festival actors and conduct the first month of rehearsals in Stratford.

I went up to Stratford for auditions. A number of actors I suggested for some of the parts also proved unavailable. But Allegra Fulton, who had performed in the workshop some ten years earlier, agreed to play Miss Edwina. She was not in the Festival company but had friends she could stay with. We saw a number of interesting actors and eventually cast Nigel Bennett as Tennessee. He was too big and a Brit, but he had maturity, experience, wit, and a good energy. He had spent most of his professional life on the East Coast and was looking to make a mark in a meaty role in Toronto. Carmen Grant would play Rose. She was also too big, but she was quick to cotton on to the changeable moods of Tennessee's beloved sister. Finally, we cast Harrison Thomas, Lucy Peacock's son, as the hustler. He was a good-looking lad, obviously talented and keen. He was a student at Ryerson, but somehow David prevailed upon his teachers to let him undertake the role.

During the month of September, I journeyed to Stratford every weekend to attend rehearsals of what was essentially a workshop. The festival generously provided us with rehearsal space, as all of their shows had now opened. Both Allegra and Harrison had to commute. Nigel and Carmen were still performing, as was David, so we had to work around their schedules. We paid the actors

Equity minimum wages for those four weeks. David demanded rewrites every week, especially of the last two or three scenes. I found this difficult because I didn't always know what he wanted, and several times said I didn't understand what he expected me to accomplish. He was patient but persistent. Finally he said, "In the final scene, in the last moments of his life, I want Tennessee to break down completely and admit his failures not so much as an artist, but as a human being. You know, you might be Tennessee. Okay, you don't have his talent, but you have his sensitivity, his insecurity, his sense of his inability to give the people he loved what they needed. You have to dig down into yourself and unlock those feelings." I went back and produced a revised ending which combined what had been the last three scenes. We rehearsed the new script and David said, "All right, I'm satisfied. We have a script. Now we rehearse it."

One of the problems for Hart House Theatre was the lack of rehearsal space. I therefore made a deal with the Metropolitan United Church, whose minister, Malcolm Sinclair, was a friend, to rehearse in their church house. I attended some of these rehearsals, but as producer, I had other matters to attend to. I persuaded four wealthy friends, including my brother, to invest in the show, setting it up with my lawyer and accountant so they would receive a full tax writeoff. This covered about half the budget. The provost of Trinity, Andy Orchard, agreed to give a cocktail party on opening night and we signed up about fifty people at a premium price to attend. We threw a similar party at Hart House on the second night, mainly for theatre people. I called friends and acquaintances and sent out invitations and emails to build an audience. There was a lot of paper, but we managed to play to houses of about three hundred people a night.

Meanwhile, I had the physical production to deal with. What I thought would be a very simple staging became, in David's hands, quite complicated. We hired his long-time collaborator Glenn Davidson to design and light the show. He envisioned the piece set in a sea of white draperies. Glenn was able to borrow the fabric and the costumes so that the main cost to us consisted of cleaning bills. David wanted to project images of Williams and his work on the set. My long-time friend Bernard Leroux put together an ever-shifting collage of family photographs interspersed with brief cuts from some of Williams' films: *A Streetcar Named Desire; Suddenly, Last Summer; Cat on a Hot Tin Roof; Night of the Iguana*. This effect, along with Glenn's constantly shifting lighting plot, created a world both surreal and dreamlike. I remembered the comment of one of the members of the New York audience that she wanted to see evidence of Williams' work. The projections went some way towards providing this element.

As producer, I was concerned to see we could get all these complex effects up and running in the short time we had for technical rehearsals. It turned out that the theatre was dark for the week preceding the show, so we were able to get an extra three days of rehearsal in the theatre. The show was ready by opening night.

The provost's party put much of the audience in a festive mood in spite of inclement weather, and the show was well received that night and at the three following performances. A few old friends said, "You'll have to explain to me sometime what it's all about." An encouraging number of people came up to me and said they loved the show. Most of the theatre professionals were more guarded in their comments. It seemed generally agreed that the women were the more successful performers. Perhaps their roles were better written. My friend and former mentor Brian Parker, one of the foremost Williams scholars in North America, was generally complimentary but thought the ending where the hustler reveals himself as the Angel of Death was sentimental. The critics stayed away, which I considered a blessing.

Jamie was not able to come to the show, as he had a gig in San Diego at the same time. I was just as happy not to have him at rehearsals. We had enough cooks. I showed him the video a few months later and he said, "It's well enough acted but the show lacks a spine. Your director took a linear play and treated it as a surreal fantasy. Our original concept was much stronger." I wasn't sure he was right but I was not upset by this.

I was pleased that we had finally got the show up and running and put it before an audience after ten years on the drawing board. One way and another this project ate up about a quarter of a million dollars. When I talked with David Mirvish and Aubrey Dan, who sometimes lost as much as twenty million dollars on a single show, this figure paled in comparison and gave me a sense of perspective. Had it been worth it? Certainly not from a financial point of view, but in terms of actually following through and realizing what we had set out to achieve, I believe it was. But I certainly viewed it as my last hurrah in the theatre.

COASTING

When I bought our house at 40 North Sherbourne Street, my father said to me, "Are you crazy? You'll never get your money out of it." I didn't care. Both Judy and I knew it was where we wanted to live. Her father said, "You're moving into a slum and your kids will be run down by traffic." But he gave us five thousand dollars and, with the five thousand dollars my father had given us as a wedding present, we were able to make the down payment. The houses around us were mainly rooming houses but our house had been re-converted to a single family dwelling, so that we did not have to spend a lot of money on renovations. I was able to pay off the mortgage using the interest I received from my Buntin Reid shares within five years, and we lived in the house happily enough for the next forty-five years.

During that time we did a good deal of entertaining. We gave dinner parties for ten people and we gained a reputation as excellent cooks. We gave cast parties after every show I directed, most of which went on till three or four in the morning. We gave parties for our children and their friends. One of the most memorable was for Guy's eighteenth birthday. Guy was taken out to dinner by a few buddies and returned to find about forty of his friends gathered in our living room. I suggested to Judy that we go out for a drink at the Park Plaza. We returned two hours later to find the house occupied by about a hundred and fifty people. It turned out Branksome Hall, about a block away, was having a formal dance that evening, and a considerable number of their students and their swains called in at our party on their way home and stayed on into the wee small hours. Judy and I went to bed on the third floor.

The next morning, I came downstairs to find one reveller asleep under the dining room table, a little girl weeping on the stairs, and one or two of Guy's friends disconsolately trying to mop the kitchen floor, which had been stained by bedraggled crepe-paper streamers. I sent the lot of them home and started to do a clean up. At about nine-thirty, the doorbell rang and I was confronted by a middle-aged man, rather the worse for wear. "Say, that was some party you guys gave last night. Next week I'm going to give a party at my place just like that. There wouldn't be any Scotch left, would there?"

In the early years of the new century, after all the kids had left home, I said to Judy every fall, "I think we should put the house up for sale in the spring." After a year or two, she said, "Every autumn you say this, but come spring, you don't do it, so I don't want to hear any more about it." I replied, "Okay, I'll tell you what. In the spring of 2008, we will both be seventy-five, and we will have been married for fifty years. We'll put the house up for sale then and move into an apartment."

In the early winter of that year I began looking at possible locations. I met my friend Ben Solway, an aging realtor, at a party and told him I was looking to sell the house but needed a place to move to.

"What about the Manulife Centre?'

"Perfect, but I've talked to them and there's nothing available."

"Leave it with me." He called a few days later to say we could move into a corner suite on an upper floor of the Manulife on the first of July.

"Then you can have the listing." Ben brought on board a younger woman to work with him. She reorganized the decor somewhat and said they wanted to show the house throughout a ten-day period. Judy and I decamped to Montreal and when we returned, they had an offer for about forty times the original cost of the house. My son Guy thought we should hold out for a higher price, but I was satisfied. We had received an offer for what I thought the house was worth, all cash, and we would not have to vacate till the end of August. We closed the deal at the end of the month. Two months later, the stock market crashed. As we had put the money into treasury bills rather than the market, we did not lose one-third of it. More luck than good management.

For our fiftieth wedding anniversary, we gave a huge party for friends, relatives, neighbours, former students, and various associates. People came from Niagara, Montreal, Calgary, Los Angeles, and New York. It was a bright, sunny afternoon and the garden was in full bloom. Our children made speeches and presented us with a copy of *Kings in Nomania*, the children's play in which Judy and I had first met at the age of ten. It was a fitting climax to our time in south Rosedale and gave us a great send-off.

Our son Ben came up from California for a week to help us move. In fact, he stayed for six weeks. He would get up every morning and go to the dump at six, go to Goodwill at eight, then pick me up at ten, and we would go to Ikea to buy shelving and other household items. We sent a good deal of stuff to Ritchies, for which we got meagre prices. Soon after, they went bankrupt, still owing us eight hundred dollars. This taught me that it was unlikely we could make any money selling our "treasures" and that it was better to give them away to people who would appreciate them.

I gave my theatre books to the Stratford Conservatory and my papers to the Fisher Library and received substantial tax receipts. Meanwhile, Ben installed us in our new quarters. He proved to be extremely handy, putting together shelves and kitchen cabinets, doing minor repairs to furniture, organizing the move. When he left, our apartment was in working order, the pictures were hung, the remaining books shelved, and the dishes and glassware stored in cupboards or displayed in cabinets. We were ready to start our new life on the thirty-fourth floor.

The Manulife proved to be wonderfully convenient. We could get anything we needed — groceries, drugs, books, liquor — without leaving the building. We were on both subway lines and could access them in bad weather without going outside. There was even a movie theatre just downstairs. Because we were right in the heart of the city, I rarely went any distance without meeting someone I knew. I gave my car to Ben. I had driven fifty years in Toronto without killing anyone and decided to quit while I was ahead; I certainly didn't miss driving in the city's increasingly complicated and dysfunctional traffic. Best of all was our view of the city. We could see the lake from our windows and the sunrises and sunsets were stunning. We had made the move at the right time, and, as it turned out, none too soon.

When I was first asked by Lyman Henderson to join the Arts and Letters Club in the early '90s, I thought, "This is a club for silly old farts," and I declined. When I was asked again, this time by Brian Parker a decade later, my opinion of the club had not changed but I thought, "Now I'll fit right in," and I did.

I discovered that a number of my friends were members and I made quite a few new friends. I would go to lunch once a week on Literary Tuesdays or Music Wednesdays and occasionally to other events. At the end of the first year, I said to Julian Mulock, who was then president, "You have some accomplished painters, the standards of the speakers and musicians are high, but your theatre productions are dreadful." To which he replied, "Why don't you do something better?"

I decided to do a production of a late Noël Coward comedy, *A Song at*

Twilight. I thought it would appeal to the members and would be manageable, as it had only one set and three actors.

I had no difficulty persuading my friend Jamie Mainprize to play the aging homosexual playwright, and I cast club members Kay Montgomery and Betty Trott as the two women. Both would become good friends. I think they were surprised when I announced that we were going to do a full production for four performances. It seemed to take them forever to learn their lines but by opening night they were ready. To the surprise of the executive, all four performances sold out, partly because Jamie had a big fan base, who turned out in force. The production was praised and I was asked what I wanted to do next.

During the next several years, I did other short plays: Edward Albee's *The American Dream*; Tennessee Williams's *The Lady of Larkspur Lotion* and *Something Unspoken*; and another Noël Coward piece, *Come into the Garden, Maud*. None of these productions drew as big houses, but I was able to maintain the standard of the first show, repeatedly drawing on the very small cadre of real actors who were club members. Because there was no money, no stage management, and very little technical help, I usually had to do all this work myself. Every time I did a show at the club, I vowed I would never do another, but it gave me something to think about other than the increasing complications attendant on old age, so I suppose it had some therapeutic value.

As well as the plays mentioned above, I wrote and directed two short Shakespearean spoofs, one a musical version of *Macbeth* with my lyrics set to tunes by Gilbert and Sullivan. Following Shakespeare's dramaturgy, my play opens with the three witches:

> Three little ghouls from Glasgow, we
> Out for a night of witchery
> Filled to the brim with ghoulish glee.
> Three little ghouls from hell.
> Eye of newt and toe of frog
> Splash of Chivas Regal in the old eggnog
> Tomorrow we'll need some hair of dog
> Three little ghouls from hell.
> Three little ghouls out looking for trouble
> Fire burn and cauldron bubble

Okay, sisters, let's pour a double,
Three little ghouls from hell.

Before he is murdered, King Duncan sings the following to the tune of the Major-General's song from *The Pirates of Penzance*:

I am the very model of a modernistic royal.
I can cool down politicians or bring them to the boil.
I tip the servants handsomely, support all local charities,
I know all the Spice Girls' hits and I collect erotic rarities.
I pitch the first ball of the season, attend fundraising dinners,
Outsmart TV interviewers and at Ascot pick the winners.
I can sit through long soliloquies and lengthy perorations
By boring foreign diplomats at the United Nations.
I've experienced love and lust, and wonder which is crueller
In short I am an utterly exemplary ruler.

One other lyric set to the Captain's song from *H.M.S. Pinafore*:

Is this a dagger that I spy
The handle towards my hand?
It's exceedingly suggestive
But it leaves me feeling restive.
I adore my little bride
But I'm not up for regicide.
Of course it's very plain
Over Scotland I could reign
With my wife, brave as a beagle,
Though her schemes are quite illegal
She's regal as an eagle
Yes regal, but illegal
Her schemes are just a tad illegal

So give a cheer and shout hurrah
For my shady lady from Panama
She can wiggle her hips and shake her booty

She's no beauty but a really hot patootie.

The other show was based on the premise that Hamlet meets Eliza Doolittle and had lyrics set to tunes from *My Fair Lady*. Here is Hamlet soliloquizing:

I'm just an ordinary prince
One whose agenda is quite plain
I want to wallow in a welter of misery and pain.
A simple prince am I
A bit like Oedipus
I simply can't abide
Undignified
Hyped-up hysterical feminine fuss and muss
Just an ordinary prince.

GERTRUDE:
Who is this fellow? He hath a goodly aspect.

HAMLET.
Oh, God, she's off again. Mother, thou hast my father much offended.

GERTRUDE.
Thy father lay about snoozing all day,
I simply put him out of his misery.

HAMLET.
Then you admit it? Oh, shame, where is thy blush?
Rush you so rashly to the rank sweat of an enseamed bed?

GERTRUDE.
Oh, grow up, Hamlet. What's your name, big boy?

DOOLITTLE.
Doolittle.

GERTRUDE.
Not very promising. I would thou couldst do much.

DOOLITTLE.
Well, I suppose I could give it a go. What'd you fancy, lady?

GERTRUDE (*sings*).
Come with me to a room somewhere
Far away from this dismal lair
We could have a brief affair
Oh would not that be lovely?

DOOLITTLE.
There's a loft over me garage
If you give me a nice massage.
I would soon have such courage
That I would treat you loverly

GERTRUDE.
I could make you feel so absolutely sublime.

DOOLITTLE.
To please you I'd gladly put in a spot of overtime.
I will leave you wanting just one more

GERTRUDE.
So then what are we waiting for?
Grab your hat and it's out the door.

BOTH.
We'll be so lovey-doverly.

Obviously a reversion to the days when I was editing *Salterrae* at Trinity College in the '50s. But some of my friends considered it the best work I had ever done. So much for literary pretensions.

Shortly after the University announced that it was going to shut down

Hart House Theatre, Janet Bessey, who had been managing the theatre as a rental facility, retired and was succeeded by Paul Templin, who decided that the theatre should once again stage a season of plays during the winter. He started off by approaching David Gardner to direct a production of *Macbeth* and he asked me if I would like to direct something. I offered to stage a joint production with the Arts and Letters Club, pointing out that in the years between the wars, Hart House Theatre had had a very close association with the club, which supplied actors like the Massey brothers, Raymond and Vincent; set designers such as Lawren Harris and J.E.H. Macdonald; and music composed by Healey Willan.

I chose Timothy Findley's *The Stillborn Lover*, and the cast included Thomas Gough, Kay Montgomery, and Malcolm Sinclair from the club, as well as some younger actors who turned up to audition. The play was hailed as the best production of the year in the *Varsity*, but the attendance was thin. I was asked to do another show the following season and decided to remount Jim Bartley's *Stephen and Mr. Wilde* with a cast of young actors mostly unknown to me. Again the show was well-received but not very heavily attended.

A year later, I was approached by my friend Peter Russell to see if I would be interested in directing a script titled *Conrad* written by James Bacque. I had known Jim when we were undergraduates at Trinity, and his pretty wife, Elizabeth, had been at Havergal with Judy. The script concerned a high-flying businessman who had been jailed for fraud and was in the process of trying to buy the prison he was incarcerated in. The reference to Lord Black was obvious. In the play, he is visited in a dream by the headmaster of his old school and in reality by his ditzy wife.

I thought the piece had potential. I suggested to Jim that in the second act, his hero should be visited by his old friend, a female former British Prime Minister. Jim wrote the second act and some lyrics for opening and closing songs.

Peter undertook to produce the show if I would direct it. Jim's idea was that it might be a joint production between the Badminton and Racquet Club, of which he was a member, and the Arts and Letters Club. In an initial meeting, the head of the program committee of the B&R was enthusiastic. Then she took the proposal to her executive, who promptly vetoed it, because they knew very well the real subject of Jim's satire was extremely litigious. They also alerted the executive of the A&L, who took a similar position. But these worthies had not reckoned on the tenacity of Peter Russell. He hired the George Ignatieff Theatre of Trinity College and we proceeded to rehearse, mainly in my living room. Fortunately, Jim and Elizabeth had moved to Penetang, so I did not have to deal with him at all our rehearsals.

I cast the show from stalwarts of the Arts and Letters Club, including Thomas Gough as Conrad. He did not look anything like the tycoon he was portraying, but I had long ago realized that if an actor can somehow grasp the essence of a real-life character, the physical resemblance is not all that important. My friend Kay Montgomery gave a virtuoso performance as Lady Thrasher, the British Prime Minister, and the rest of the cast were at least serviceable. Peter mounted a highly successful advertising campaign and we played to full houses for three nights. The show garnered so much attention that we revived it several weeks later, again playing to full houses. Peter had kept a firm hand on the finances and all the participants received a handsome honorarium. It was instructive to me to realize how much success in the theatre depends on timeliness and an edgy presentation, something that would not have been news to either W. Shakespeare or G. B. Shaw.

I was invited by the new warden of Hart House to attend a committee that she had put together of mainly businessmen and lawyers, whom she hoped would raise seven million dollars to revamp the theatre. Some of them were optimistic, although I thought this would be a very hard sell, which was confirmed when I approached several philanthropic theatre lovers including Hal Jackman and John McKellar. We collected perhaps $500,000. Then the market crashed. I realized that this was now an impossible sell. I advised Louise to forget about renovation and instead hire a smart, young artistic director, the first since I had resigned thirty years earlier. I pointed out that the obvious choice was a young man named Jeremy Hutton, who had already staged vigorous and colourful productions of *Romeo and Juliet* and *Othello*.

I'm not sure how much weight my counsel carried, but in fact Jeremy was hired, backed up by Doug Floyd as general manager. They proved a workable team, bringing the theatre back on track and building audiences. I was recently able to convince our foundation to fund a visiting actor for three years. The first was David Ferry, who, under Jeremy's direction, played Shannon in Tennessee Williams' *The Night of the Iguana* to good houses in the spring of 2012.

Shortly before we sold our house on Sherbourne Street, my friends Andrew Watson and Margaret MacMillan invited me to be a member of

Senior Common Room at Trinity College. Margaret was a long-time friend of Andrew's and I had known her casually for some time when she was a history professor at Ryerson. She wrote the book *Paris 1919* about the armistice negotiations following the 1914–18 World War, which she was unable to get published in Canada. She sent it to an English publisher who accepted it, and it won two major British literary prizes. As always with a Canadian writer who receives major recognition outside the country, she was immediately catapulted to celebrity back home, and shortly thereafter she was elected the first woman provost of Trinity College.

I found I knew a few of the members of the Senior Common Room and fairly quickly formed an acquaintance with a number of others. The food served at their dinners was palatable, the wine flowed, and they gave enjoyable special dinners at Christmas, the Conversat before the annual college formal dance, and at the end of spring term. The conversation at these functions was often amusing, though not particularly intellectual, and rather concerned with current politics, where to stay when travelling, and academic gossip.

Not long after this, I was invited to become an associate of Massey College by the master, John Fraser, whom I had known when he was a drama critic and journalist. John was at once genial and peppery. When he was touted as the master of Massey, I was skeptical, but in fact he stepped into the shoes of Robertson Davies with ease and reactivated the social and cultural life of the college in his own style. As with Hart House, the Masseys had donated the college to the University but not endowed it. The University was loath to channel funds into what was patently an elitist institution. Davies had appointed a few wealthy friends like Walter Gordon and Claire and Amy Stewart as honorary senior fellows.

John Fraser could hardly appoint his five hundred most intimate acquaintances as fellows. Instead, he formed what he called the Quadrangle Society and recruited a large number of members, who for a certain minimum but not overly onerous annual contribution would be invited to dinners, lectures, book club readings, and a variety of other activities. The members of the Quadrangle Society were of such eminence that had the college been bombed while they were all in attendance at some function, at least half the social and cultural establishment of Toronto would have been eliminated.

I was occasionally introduced, when I spoke publicly, as a theatrical historian, I suppose on the strength of my Stratford book. This amused me, as

I thought how disapprovingly my old colleagues at the Drama Centre would react to this sudden elevation to their ranks: a half-page bibliography and no footnotes. It seemed logical to follow up my limited success with another book in the same general area, and my co-workers on *Romancing the Bard* had a project ready and waiting.

Ramsay Derry had been instrumental in persuading the McLean Foundation to buy up all Grant Macdonald's theatrical drawings from his estate upon his death and present them to the Agnes Etherington Art Centre at Queen's University in Kingston. Macdonald was a gifted draughtsman and portraitist who had spent a good deal of time in London and New York from the mid-'30s to the early '50s and had drawn every major stage and screen performer before retiring to Kingston. He had also drawn all the major players at Stratford in the early years of the Festival. Ramsay and John Lee, who had contributed the highly original and effective design for my Stratford book, had long had a plan to bring out a book of Macdonald's theatrical drawings. John would design it, I would write the text, and Ramsay would edit it.

However, we were unable to agree about the tone of the text for the book and the project eventually foundered. We did, however, succeed in mounting a show of the drawings in Stratford, Toronto, and Kingston.

At the same time, I had begun work on a book of profiles of Canadian theatrical performers from Beatrice Lillie to Adrienne Clarkson. I had seen all of the people I was writing about many times, and I had a personal connection with all of them, sometimes slight and tenuous, sometimes quite extensive. I discussed the project with Kirk Howard at Dundurn, and he expressed interest but suggested the project needed a subsidy, perhaps ten thousand dollars, to pay for photographs. I was not immediately successful in raising money for this project and so it moved to the back burner. A few years later, I decided that it might be revived if I added some more contemporary performers. I now have a contract for the book, the text is written, and I am working with John Lee to assemble pictures to illustrate it, which, because of the need to get permissions, is proving a much more formidable task than I anticipated. I also have a promise of a substantial donation from David Mirvish.

I don't remember when I first had the idea of writing a memoir. Marq de Villiers suggested I write a book of travel pieces and I put together an outline of possible destinations. I know I discussed this with Ramsay Derry and it may have been he who decided me to shift my focus. I wanted to explore some of the worlds I had experienced in my youth: the rural simplicity of my grandparents, the shenanigans I shared with my friend Dick in suburban North Toronto, the magical excitement of being a child actor, the more or less madcap life I led as an undergraduate, the silliness of my experience as a naval cadet, my disillusionment at my first experience of Europe. I also wanted to write about some of the remarkable people I knew when I was growing up: Kay Williams, Dorothy Goulding, Herbert Whittaker, Robert Gill, and Philip Child, among others. I received encouragement from a number of mentors and commentators: Stan Bevington, Dorothy-Jane Needles, and Jan Walters. Stan, whom I had known since he came to Buntin Reid as a prospective customer looking for credit, which we gave him, was particularly enthusiastic.

Although the editor of Coach House Books rejected the manuscript I sent Stan, he told me he would find me a publisher, and he did: Michael Holmes at ECW Press. I chose as a title *Young Hunting*. I threw a big party at Trinity, and we sold over a hundred books at the launch. Michael thought the book might take off but it didn't. We could not manage to get notices in the major dailies in spite of John Fraser offering to review it in the *Globe and Mail*. We did receive favourable mention in *Quill & Quire*, on Shelagh Rogers' CBC Radio show, and in the *Literary Review of Canada*, but the initial run did not sell out. I came to understand that the only authors who sold well in Canada were those who had received recognition in Britain or the United States, unless they were writing about politics. Michael expressed an interest in a second volume, and I duly sent him another manuscript. After some hesitation, he sent me a contract and it appeared in 2013 under the title *Still Hunting*. This is the third volume and takes me up to the present. Hopefully it will find as favourable a response from readers as the first two volumes.

One morning, I received a call from Marian Hebb, a lawyer specializing in literary projects, to tell me that Scott Symons had died. He had specified in his will that he wanted a funeral mass. "I don't know how to organize this. I don't know any of the family or anything." I assured her that I could do what was necessary. I phoned Scott's brother, Tom, to inform him. "Thank you for letting me know, Martin," he said and hung up. I then phoned David Neelands at Trinity, and he agreed to arrange the funereal at St. Thomas, a church near the university, which apparently Scott had attended. Could I supply pallbearers? I lined up three old friends of Scott's and also phoned John Fraser, who agreed to host a small reception after the funeral in the

Massey College common room. The funeral was attended by more people than I had anticipated. There were two additional pallbearers, Stan Bevington and a youngish man named Marc Côté. After the service Marc and I had a conversation and discovered we had other friends in common besides Scott. We agreed to meet for lunch.

Our lunch was highly convivial and we exchanged a good deal of gossip. It turned out that Marc was a publisher. He knew I was a writer and asked if he could see some of my work. I readily agreed. I told him about the profiles and the memoir, but he seemed more interested in my short stories. I had been writing sporadically since my teens: plays and screenplays, but also short prose pieces. Most of these just sat in a drawer, but a year or so before I met Marc I had begun to go back and review some of them, including pieces I had written as much as forty years before. Much of it seemed like junk, but there were some stories that I thought worth reworking. I was able to give Marc a couple of manuscripts, and he came back to me to say that he thought one or two of them were quite good and some of the others could be publishable with additional work. I sent him about fifteen stories in all and he offered me a contract. I was somewhat surprised but pleased and set to work revising under his supervision. Twelve of the stories were published in 2013 under the title *The Critic and Other Stories*. I still have more stories and a novel based on the TV series I drafted for Tim Bond.

Although we were pleased with our life at the Manulife Centre, it was clear to me that Judy's health was deteriorating. We still had people over for drinks and sometimes dinner, but these occasions became increasingly infrequent. Judy went to see various specialists and was diagnosed with congestive heart failure. Her digestive tract was also malfunctioning. In the spring of 2012, she took to her bed and was no longer able to walk. We discovered that OHIP would provide us with a hospital bed, weekly visits from a nurse, and daily visits from a care worker. We also hired two additional caregivers. Judy still had all her marbles and was not in pain, but she needed an increasing amount of attention. I came to see that writing was a good way for me to concentrate on something other my personal situation.

For me, 2013 turned out to be a sort of annus mirabilis. On January first, I was awarded the Order of Canada; in February, the Queen's Diamond Jubilee Medal; and in June, the University of Toronto's Arbor Award. I also turned 80 and had a huge birthday party at Hart House attended by about 150 people, some of whom I'd known for seventy years, others for perhaps six weeks — a mix of friends, relatives, former students, and theatrical associates. My granddaughter Eleanor Hart sang a song, for which I had written the lyrics, accompanied by my friend John Roby, who wrote the music. I launched my two new books, *Still Hunting* and *The Critic*. Neither book received any media attention but a good many friends said they enjoyed them.

In June, I went to visit my son Ben in California. A reading was held of our play *The Gentleman Caller*, directed by Ben's former girlfriend Lauren Campedelli. Robert Joy, whom I had directed as a student and later a professional, gave a splendidly wry, witty, and moving performance as Tennessee Williams. We played to a packed house of 60 people who applauded enthusiastically, and a full performance in Los Angeles seemed a distinct possibility.

Then in November, John Roby and I workshopped a revised version of *Baby Grand* with Nora McLellan, preparing for a full-scale production, probably in 2015. This was followed by a sort of backers' audition in July of 2014 in the cabaret space of the Buddies in Bad Times Theatre. Nora was not available and we were able to get a replacement, Jackie Richardson, who was sensational. It seems possible that we may be able to get up a full production with Jackie playing the title role of Baby. I had thought I was through with the theatre, but as my friend Ann Stuart remarked, "Maybe the theatre isn't through with you."

Now in my eighties, I look back on a full and varied life. I have had the opportunity to experience many interesting situations and people. Although many people think I am as rich as Croesus, I can no longer afford to travel or even drive a car, but I don't mind. My family keeps on saying how lucky I am to be an artist. I don't consider I have been much of an artist. I have rather been a facilitator. My greatest talent has been bringing people together. And if I have made a contribution, it has been in giving people opportunities: as a businessman, as a teacher and director of young people, and more recently through the K. M. Hunter Artist Awards. If I look back on my life with some sense of accomplishment, that is what gives me a lasting sense of satisfaction.

Judy died in September 2015, a few weeks short of her eighty-second birthday. We had been married for fifty-seven years and known each other for over seventy. As with any marriage, there were some ups and downs. We had an active sex life for some fifteen years that gradually waned, but we remained best friends for all of that time. Judy was an elegant and vivacious woman with a sharp sense of humour but also great generosity and spirit. She was an accomplished storyteller and a perceptive but never malicious critic. When we were young we were both interested in the arts, particularly theatre and music. In her mature years, Judy became a highly respected kindergarten teacher, primarily in the inner city of Toronto. For over twenty-five years, she did much to help underprivileged kids, encouraging their interest in the arts and championing them against sometimes unsympathetic and abusive parents. In her later years she took a strong interest in conservation, especially projects involving wild animals and endangered species. Our interests had diverged, but we still had dinner together most nights and enjoyed an active social life. I cannot imagine what my life would have been without her.

I am not completely housebound, but I have no desire to stray very far from home. I realize I was lucky to be born and to grow up when I did, when the worst horrors of the twentieth century were over. As I came of age, the economy was expanding and opportunities were opening up. I don't envy the young people of today, for all the variety their lives encompass. I am not hip but I am comfortable. Once in a while I go to a play, a movie, a party. I talk on the telephone to a few old friends. I sit and read, listen to recorded music: Bach, Mozart, Chopin, jazz from the '20s, '30s, and '40s. Asleep, I dream fantastic dreams, always trying to get somewhere, striving to overcome impossible obstacles, seeking to make order out of chaos. Awake, I still scribble a bit or sit and daydream, the dreams of an old man who always wanted too much, but managed to get quite a bit. Managed to savour quite a lot of the variety life has to offer.